NEW RULES
OF THE GAME

Published by CelebrityPress™, Orlando, FL
A division of The Celebrity Branding Agency®

Celebrity Branding® is a registered trademark
Printed in the United States of America.

ISBN#: 978-0-9853643-9-7
LCCN#: 2012941085

This publication is designed to provide accurate and authoritative information with regard to the subject matter covered. It is sold with the understanding that the publisher is not engaged in rendering legal, accounting, or other professional advice. If legal advice or other expert assistance is required, the services of a competent professional should be sought. The opinions expressed by the authors in this book are not endorsed by CelebrityPress™ and are the sole responsibility of the author rendering the opinion.

Most CelebrityPress™ titles are available at special quantity discounts for bulk purchases for sales promotions, premiums, fundraising, and educational use. Special versions or book excerpts can also be created to fit specific needs.

For more information, please write:

CelebrityPress™
520 N. Orlando Ave, #2
Winter Park, FL 32789
or call 1.877.261.4930

Visit us online at www.CelebrityPressPublishing.com

NEW RULES
OF THE GAME

Contents

CHAPTER 1

Millionaire Matrix

By Robert G. Allen

Deep down, most of us long for a world like our mother's womb where as babies, we were cradled in comfort and fed constantly through her umbilical cord. As soon as we enter the world, we're rudely slapped on the rear to get us to take our first crying breath. Some of us have been crying ever since.

As soon as we're old enough, we get thrown out of the nest, and are left on our own to fend for ourselves. Many of us are unconsciously looking for another mothership where we can plug our umbilical cords back in and return to being fed.

We're programmed from birth to believe that the most respectable, stable and secure way to earn money and support a family is to find a job and work on someone else's mothership.

Working for someone else is an honorable way to earn a living. Billions of people do it every day. However, a few of us chafe at the thought of working for another person. We know we were destined for something grander.

We don't want to *work* on someone's mothership. We want to *own* a mothership.

The difference between *owning* a mothership and *working* on a mothership is huge.

There are two radically different mindsets. Employees on the mother-ship usually work on the "hourly" plan. They earn X dollars per every hour of work. They punch in at the beginning of the day and punch out at the end. The apparent advantage to this kind of lifestyle is that it offers you a steady salary with benefits.

By the way, the word salary comes from the Latin root word "salarium," which means salt allowance. In ancient Rome, soldiers were paid part of their wages in salt. This gave rise to the expression, "not worth his salt."

Do you want to work for salt money?

Working on someone's mothership is a matter of security—salary, benefits, stability.

Owning a mothership is a matter of freedom—sales, profits, risk.

There are two doors in life: the door marked "Security" and the door marked "Freedom."

If you choose the one marked "Security," you lose it and your free-dom.

The security game is an illusion. There is no such thing. You might rent yourself out to work on someone's mothership for a while, but the safest path is to own your stream of income. Most people trade their time for dollars. You need to trade your time for profits.

This is a very different mindset: the entrepreneurial one. Are you an entrepreneur?

Entrepreneurs don't hold traditional jobs. Their job is to create jobs.

If you long for the freedom of the entrepreneurial lifestyle, get ready to make a break—but not until you've figured out how to replace your steady flow of paychecks from your salary with a stream of income from your profits.

WORKING ON A MOTHERSHIP VS. OWNING A MOTHERSHIP

There are only 168 hours in a week. You direct many of these hours toward earning money. Suppose your dream is to earn $100,000 a year. At $10 an hour, you'd have to work every single hour of every single day for the entire year to even get close to it. At this rate, you'd work yourself to death for under a hundred grand. If you worked the normal forty-hour work week, your hourly salary would need to be at least FIFTY DOLLARS AN HOUR in order to earn the same $100,000. This is how salary people think when they talk about money. They rent themselves out by the hour.

How much did you earn at your VERY first job? A dollar an hour? Then, when did you graduate to $10 per hour? Eventually, your skills increase and your pay does, too. You scale up to a higher salary. Have you broken $20 an hour? $30 an hour? $50 an hour? Fifty dollars an hour at 40 hours a week times 50 weeks comes to about $100,000 per year. If you're a salaried worker, it's hard to crack that number.

Profit-focused people talk about money in an entirely different way. They generally refer to profit per unit. Or profit per deal. Or profit per transaction. Since there are almost seven billion people on Planet Earth, there are almost seven billion potential customers. And new customers are being born every day. The possibilities are limitless.

There is an Ashleigh Brilliant cartoon which illustrates this perfectly. The caption reads,

"I'm not greedy: I'd be quite satisfied with just one dollar from every person in the country."

At a profit of a dollar per unit, you'd need to sell 100,000 widgets this year. At ten dollars profit, you'd need to sell 10,000 widgets. At a hundred dollars profit, you'd only need to sell a thousand. Making $100,000 a year in the entrepreneurial world, although not easy, is certainly doable. It could be as simple as doing one great real estate deal. Or marketing a $5,000 yearly coaching program to 20 people. I've actually earned a hundred thousand dollars in a single hour!!!!!!

(Of course, it took me 30 years to figure out how to do it.)

The first shift you need to make is from thinking about hours to thinking about profits. Then ask yourself, how can I create some product, service, idea or experience that generates a consistent profit?

There are at least three major paths to prosperity. Instead of salaries, you want to earn profits. Profits are earned by "selling stuff." Three kinds of stuff:

Products =   Stuff

Services =   Doing stuff for someone

Information = Teaching someone to do stuff

Successfully launching a business can be challenging. As soon as you're earning a profit, then the secret is to learn to how to scale up and scale down.

What does it mean to "scale up"? It means to market more units in magnitudes of 10.

$1 PROFIT PER UNIT

If your profit per unit is $1, you need to sell 100,000 units per year to earn $100,000. That's a large number. You might not believe yourself able to do that. To make that number more manageable, let's scale it down into bite-sized chunks. 100,000 units would break down to about 8,000 units a month. Or 2,000 units per week. Or about 300 units per 24 hours. Or about 12 units an hour.

When you scale it down to an hourly number, it sounds much more feasible. Hmmmmm, you ask yourself. I wonder how I could market 12 units per hour?

$10 PROFIT PER UNIT

Let's scale up the profit per unit, to $10. Let's assume you had an excellent widget with a $10 profit. Could you sell one of them to somebody this month? Sure. No problem.

Let's scale the number up further. Could you sell ten this month?

You're not all that excited about selling, but sure, you can imagine finding ten people you know who might buy one each. That's about two or three a week.

Could you sell ten this week? Hmmmm…that might take a bit more thinking. You'd probably need to work harder at it to sell one or two a day, but it's possible.

How about ten a day?

"That would be a full time job," you think. "I'd probably have to hire someone to help me sell them. Or maybe I'd launch a website. But, yes, if I REALLY, REALLY, REALLY wanted to sell ten a day, I guess I could figure out a way to do it."

Hmmmm…ten a day is 300 each month. At $10 profit per unit, that comes to $3,000 a month. If you translate that into "salary" language, that's about $20 an hour. It might not be worth quitting your day job. There's got to be a better way.

Well, you've got several choices. You could scale up the number of units you sell per day. How about 100 a day? That would generate $30,000 a month. Would that make it worthwhile for you to quit your day job? Well, yeah! Duh! $30,000 a month would add up to over $350,000 a year!

How could you sell 100 of those a day? Can you imagine it? You'd probably need a sales force. A company. Employees. Offices. Warehouses. But, yes. It could be done.

Your other choice would be to scale up the profit per unit. Do you think you could sell some product, service or information that would net you about $100 per unit?

$100 PROFIT PER UNIT

Could you sell one unit a month for $100 profit? Hmmmm. Probably.

How about one a week? Could you do that?

"Hmmmm," you say. "That might take some thinking. I could probably fit it into my post-work hours. One unit a week. Sure." How about a unit a day?

"Now, that would be harder. That would take some serious thinking. How much could I make? One unit a day times $100 profit per unit times 30 days. That's about $3,000 a month. Nope. That doesn't entice me."

But what about ten units a day, which would make you about a thousand bucks a day? Could you handle that?

"$1000 a day? $30,000 a month? $365,000 a year? From only 300 units a month. Yeah, that profit level could really get me excited."

$1,000 PROFIT PER UNIT

Do you think you could sell one unit a month at a $1,000 profit? You'd have to talk to fewer people, and they'd need to be more qualified. Only one a month. Could you do it?

It depends. You'd have to have a conversation with yourself. "I'm not very good at selling. I'd have to find something I REALLY, REALLY, REALLY believed in. Something that I was convinced would REALLY, REALLY, REALLY work. It would have to be on my purpose path. But, yeah, I think I could work up my courage to sell one of those a month."

How about one a week? That's about $4,000 a month. $50,000 a year. Would that be worth your while? Would that be a step up for you or a step down?

"Hmmmm…one a week, huh? It depends on how hard it would be. Depends upon how long it would take for me to sell it. If I could do it in an hour a day…after work…that might entice me."

How about one a day? On average, that would be $30,000 a month. Would that interest you?

"Hmmmmm…where would I find the kinds of products I can make a

$1,000 profit from? I'd only have to sell 100 of those in an entire year to make $100,000. That's only eight a month. Two a week. Yeah. I think I could do that."

Well, let's scale up just for fun. How many units would you need to sell to net a million dollars a year? At $1,000 profit per unit, that would be 1,000 units. Or about three a day.

Let's go in the opposite direction. Rather than considering a unit with a $1000 profit margin, let's scale up to $10,000. Does anyone in the world buy things that expensive?

Of course. Houses. Cars. Machines. Furniture. Paintings. Animals. Professional fees. Travel. There are thousands of products and services that net high profits.

This very day, there might be 100,000 sellers worldwide who netted $10,000 in profit from some product or service.

In fact, there were probably 10,000 sellers who made $100,000 in profit from a single sale today.

Hundreds of individuals and companies made a million dollars in profit TODAY from just one sale.

There may be ten who made $10 million from a single sale today.

At least one person made $100 million dollars today.

Every day, someone makes that kind of money.

Where do you want to enter this game?

Do you want to sell a million widgets at a $1 profit?

Or do you want to sell one widget for a profit of a million dollars?

This is what I call the Millionaire Matrix. There are a million ways to earn a million dollars. I'm going to show you at least seven of them:

The Millionaire Matrix

$$1,000,000 \times \$1 = \$1,000,000$$

$$100,000 \times \$10 = \$1,000,000$$

$$10,000 \times \$100 = \$1,000,000$$

$$1,000 \times \$1,000 = \$1,000,000$$

$$100 \times \$10,000 = \$1,000,000$$

$$10 \times \$100,000 = \$1,000,000$$

$$1 \times \$1,000,000 = \$1,000,000$$

The higher the profit margin, the lower the number of units you need to sell in order to net your million. And vice versa. Do a little number-crunching. Could you sell 10,000 widgets for a profit of $100 each in your lifetime? That's an extra million dollars over the next 20 years. Or about $50,000 a year. Could you do it? Sure.

Could you do it in ten years? At the rate of 1000 units a year, or 80 a month, or 20 a week? Maybe.

Let's cut to the chase. Could you do it in a year? A million dollars in profit THIS YEAR??? You'd just have to create a product that 10,000 people would want so badly that they'd part with enough money to net you $100 per product.

The secret is to scale up and scale down the Millionaire Matrix to reach a set of numbers that make you believe you can do it. Once you reach your BELIEF number, then you develop a plan to reach your DESIRED timeframe. Do you believe you could sell 10,000 hundred-dollar widgets in a lifetime? "Yeah, I believe I can do that," you say. Would you like to make a million dollars this year? "YEAH, that would be exciting!!!!"

Pick a number you can believe. Multiply that by a burning desire. And you'll millionize your life faster than you can imagine.

This is how you "turn on your greed glands," as Gary Halbert liked to say.

IF YOU BELIEVE IT AND DESIRE IT, YOU CAN ACQUIRE IT.

Scale up the number of units sold. Scale up the profit per unit.

Then, scale down the time it takes to sell each unit. From one year to one month to one week to one day to one hour to one minute.

Then, scale down the time YOU have to be personally involved in the selling process.

I was the co-author of the very popular book called "The One Minute Millionaire." A MILLION DOLLARS in a minute! That's absolutely crazy, right? Well, think about it. How could you make a million dollars in a minute using the Millionaire Matrix? Hmmmmm. It would depend upon the database of people. Do people buy products online that cost $100 each? Absolutely. Ten thousand times a DAY. Do you think you could create a $100 product that someone would buy from YOU online?

Play along with me here...just say "yes!"

Suppose someone is willing to send you a hundred bucks for one of your widgets. How many people would you need to reach this way to earn a million dollars over a lifetime? Ten thousand people. Could you do that? Probably, if you had a lifetime to figure it out.

OK. Suppose you had a hot database of a million people who were nuts about the kind of products you're marketing. If you dangled the right kind of bait in front of this school of hungry fish, you'd probably have some takers, wouldn't you?

How many takers would you need to net you a million dollars from this pool of a million fish? Ten thousand. That's a lot. But wait. What percentage of a million is ten thousand? It's only one percent. ONE PERCENT!!!!!!

If your product was good enough, 99% of them could say no and you'd still be up a million dollars. That's totally realistic, isn't it?

How long would it take for a million people to read the email that would offer your $100 product? Less than a minute. And one percent of them might bite. That's a million dollars in one minute. Do the math. A million bucks a minute.

Let's scale up the profit margin to $1,000. Could you create something—a seminar, a one-on-one coaching session, an info-product— that would be worth a thousand bucks? It would have to be REALLY, REALLY good for someone to spend that kind of money. Let's return to our database of a million fish. How many fish would need to bite? Only a thousand! What percentage is that? One-tenth of 1%. Now, that's totally realistic! Hey, I COULD DO THAT, you think.

So now you believe it. Do you want it? Is that a yes?

Then, here's what you'll need to do.

Create some fantastic product, service or information.

Find an existing database.

Drop your bait in the water and watch what happens.

Enough theory. Let's look at a real example.

$137,000 IN 45 DAYS, STARTING FROM SCRATCH

Nicky sat in a seminar and was enamored by the numbers. It was a seminar I taught called "Cracking the Millionaire Code." And she cracked it. Here's how.

She was listening to the marketing guru Jay Abraham talk about finding a product to market. You see, you don't even need your own product. There are millions of products out there in some warehouse already, just waiting for you to come along and offer to help sell them. Talk about low-hanging fruit! It's hanging all around you.

Every business needs help selling. Some need it even more than others. Some businesses are terrible at selling. They love creating products but they're lousy at marketing them. You can come to their rescue.

Jay Abraham suggested that you find a product category that matches your purpose—things that YOU LOVE TO SELL because YOU BELIEVE in them. Enter a Google search word using your purpose path.

Let's use Google. Everyone is fighting to have their products show up in the top 100 in a Google search. Let's do just the opposite in our Google search. Instead of going to the top of a Google search, go instead to the BOTTOM. (Or past two or three hundred search results… which is farther than most people ever go.)

What does this tell you? These companies don't know how to sell their products. They need help. Search through to find a hundred or so that have some product, service or information that you really connect with…that you'd actually love to sell. Contact them and ask them if they'd like to sell you a bunch of their products—at a very low wholesale price. Maybe they've got a warehouse full of items that they'd love to get rid of. You're looking for products you can acquire for a super bargain—that you can almost steal.

How many companies would you need to contact until you found the perfect product, one that fits your purpose, at a bargain-basement, below wholesale price?

So you research a thousand companies to find a hundred possibilities to narrow down to ten possible products…or the best one percent.

Now, you don't have to warehouse this product. It's already being warehoused. You don't have to ship it. They'll ship it for you as long as you pay for it. They've already created some marketing information that you can use. It's ready to go. You haven't spent a dime and you're in control of a million dollars worth of product.

You're looking for a widget with a high-profit margin—like something that costs you $1 and has a value of over $100.

This is exactly what Nicky did. She found a company with a CD that contained special software and hundreds of valuable special reports for stay-at-home mothers. It was extremely valuable. But it only cost $1 to reproduce. Nicky acquired the unlimited, non-exclusive rights to market this CD for an investment of only $1,000.

Are you still with me?

What's the next piece of this profit puzzle?

You need people to sell it to.

Now, it's time to find an appropriate database—people who are already looking for this kind of PSI (product, service or information).

In the modern world, where the Internet reaches more than two billion people (a number that's growing by the hour) how many databases are out there? Millions of them. (A database, by the way, is just the contact information for a list of customers.) Some websites list the contact information of just the website owner. That's a database of one. Other databases gather the contact information of every customer. Some small online companies only have ten, a hundred, or a thousand customers.

That brings us to another type of matrix:

The Millionaire Database Matrix

1,000,000 databases with 1 name = 1,000,000 customers

100,000 databases with 10 names = 1,000,000 customers

10,000 databases with 100 names = 1,000,000 customers

1,000 databases with 1000 names = 1,000,000 customers

100 databases with 10,000 names = 1,000,000 customers

10 databases with 100,000 names = 1,000,000 customers

1 database with 1,000,000 names = 1,000,000 customers

What's the bottom line? How hard is it be to find 100 databases with at least 10,000 names?

Why would these database owners let you send an email to their database of highly prized customers? If YOU sent it to their list, it would be SPAM. It has to come from THEM. Why would they let you do that? You would have to arrange some sort of profit split.

Nicky searched high and low and stumbled upon two college students who had been studying database gathering in a semester computer class. These nerds had been able to gather 700,000 opt-in email addresses during a three-month semester. (We assume they got an A in the class.) They also were unaware of just how valuable their database was. Nicky partnered with them to let her send a message to their database. But there was a twist. She explained in her email that 100% of the profits…in fact ALL of the money would go to fund orphans and orphanages. She has a very soft spot in her heart for orphans.

The email went out. Here was the offer. "Send me $100 for this incredibly valuable CD. You get the CD and I'll give ALL of the money to charity. All of it. I won't keep a penny for myself."

Guess how many people on that database took her up on her offer?

1,370 people. That was less than a third of 1% of the customers on the list. 99.66% percent said "no" to her offer.

Total earnings? $137,000. Cash. Starting from nothing. Less than 45 days after learning this concept. What an enlightened "profitable servant" project!

Starting with this initial success, she and her partners have since generated over a million dollars in profit for themselves from this same list of names. How do they do it? They find profitable PSIs to offer to their database.

You have now learned this concept. How soon can you earn your first dollar?

The goal is to eventually be selling thousands of units per day without having to spend more than a few hours each month to cash the checks.

THE INFORMATION BUSINESS

Now, let's explore the secret to why this approach works so well with information products. With most "product products"—i.e., hard, lumpy objects— the cost of producing that product is AT LEAST 10%

of its price. Often, it's MUCH more than that. For example, how much does it cost General Motors to produce a car? The hard costs of metal and plastic are very expensive, before you even get to all of the labor and shipping. The profit margin per car is low. But with information products, the profit margin is EXTREMELY HIGH. Why? Because it's so inexpensive to produce them.

In the previous example, Nicky was able to find an information product that someone else had produced. It was a CD that was packed with valuable information. To the right customer, this well-organized information was worth over a hundred dollars. Yet, the cost of duplicating the CD was under a dollar. The profit margin was 99%.

In many cases, this information can be digitized and sent over the internet at lightning speed FOR FREE. If people have a serious problem and need specific information YESTERDAY, they'll pay a premium for immediate delivery.

Of all the products you can sell, information is the ultimate product.

INTELLECTUAL PROPERTY IS THE REAL ESTATE OF THE 21ST CENTURY

Another term for information is intellectual property. It's the real estate of the 21st century. It's so easy to create and sell. It's the ultimate wealth creation vehicle. That's why I say that the information business is the best business in the world.

The Benefits of Information Marketing:

It is:

- Easy to research
- Easy to create
- Easy and cheap to test
- Easy and cheap to produce, inventory and correct

It offers:

- Low start-up costs
- A high perceived value
- A high markup
- Income that's generated while you sleep
- An unlimited worldwide market
- Mobility—you can operate from any mailbox in the world
- Copyright protection from competitors
- A prestigious, impressive career ("I'm an author.")
- Personal satisfaction: leaving a permanent record for future generations
- The opportunity to make a difference

There are so many ways to create information products.

52 WAYS TO PROFIT
FROM INTELLECTUAL PROPERTY

Books
E-books
Audio Books
Audio Programs
Single Audio Cassettes
Video Trainings
Multimedia Systems
Workbooks
Coaching Programs

Mentoring & Apprenticeship Programs
Speaking Internationally
Speaking in Breakout Sessions
Speaking to Represent your Employer
Train-the-Trainer Programs
Public Seminars
Corporate Training Programs

Presenting at Large Events

Boot Camps
Tele-Boot Camps
Hourly Consulting
Long-Term Consulting
Subscription Consulting

Spokesperson Contracts
Licensing
Infomercial Products
Home Study Courses
Tele-seminars
Weekend Retreats
Subscription Audio CD Series
Ghostwriting & Co-Authoring
Branded Retail Products
Mini-Books
Trade Associations
Conventions & Trade Shows
Agenting & Information Arbitrage

Seminar Company Workshops
Business-Building Systems
Practice-Management Tools
Newsletters
Radio or TV Shows
Philanthropic Foundations
Media Expertise
Syndicated Columns

Private-Label Magazine
Rights—Yours
Rights—Other People's
Special Reports & White Papers
CD-ROM & DVD Training

Counseling Services
Adult Professional Education

Reference Guides & Directories Software

A BILLION IN SPECIALIZED KNOWLEDGE

I stumbled into the information business over 30 years ago. It started when I ran a $25 ad in my local newspaper offering a small seminar on real estate investing. I had knowledge, skill, expertise and passion for real estate, and I loved to teach. I began teaching an evening course at a local hotel in Provo, Utah. As I remember, I charged $75 for a four-week class. There were about 20 students each month, which gave me an extra $1,500 in revenue. The hotel room was cheap. The manual was collated by me and my wife in our master bedroom. It was a high profit margin.

Then, one day, I had a bright idea. I wondered if someone would pay $100 for a full-day seminar. Rather than having four weekly sessions, we could get it all done in one Saturday. I ran a simple ad in my newspaper for a free seminar on how to buy real estate with little or no money down. Many people attended, paying the enrollment fee of $100. We held more free events. Eventually, the full-day seminar was filled with about 100 people. 100 people times $100 is…Ka-Ching…TEN THOUSAND DOLLARS for a single day of teaching. (Of course, it took several days of planning and marketing.) Still, ten thousand dollars was a lot of money 30 years ago. It's a lot of money today! I had found a pure vein of gold.

I wondered how much someone would pay for a TWO-day seminar. Would they pay $195? I ran a full-page ad in the newspaper. Two hundred people ended up coming at about two hundred dollars per person. That was FORTY thousand dollars for a single weekend. We're talking serious money. I decided to scale up some more.

Of course, this sounds too easy. I've left out the hard parts—the times when NOBODY paid for the seminar. There were dozens of hard knocks and disappointments—like the time when my wife's purse was stolen when she was registering people at one of our seminars. Or the time when I invested a lot of advertising in Denver, Colorado, for a seminar held when the Denver Broncos were playing a key football game. Money down the drain.

Still, we kept scaling things up. We eventually charged $500 for a weekend seminar. Ultimately, I licensed the seminar to a nationwide outfit and scaled down my payout to a net royalty of $58.50 per student. Each week, hundreds of students nationwide paid to attend my seminar. Every Tuesday they'd send me the royalties for the previous week. The checks were for $20,000, $30,000, or even $50,000 each week. And I didn't even need to be there to teach the seminar. They eventually taught 103,000 people at about $500 per student. I just cashed the checks—millions of dollars worth of them.

During this time, I released the book, "Nothing Down: A Proven Program that Shows You How to Buy Real Estate with Little or No Money Down." Fueled by the advertising from the seminars, the book took off. It spent 58 weeks on the New York Times best-seller list.

But good things often come to an end. The seminar outfit stopped earning profits during a down time in the real estate market. They closed their doors. That major source of income dried up. Then, a freak avalanche destroyed our mountain home at the Sundance ski resort. When the insurance company balked at paying the insurance, our banker called in a large loan I had borrowed on a speculative real estate project. We went into a full financial avalanche. We lost everything…and eventually declared bankruptcy.

From nothing to everything to nothing again in seven short years. Scaling up to 100% and then scaling back down to zero. About a year later, one of my previous employees, Thomas R. Painter, tracked me down and convinced me to scale things back up again. Our first seminar was attended by 93 people at $1,000 per person. We scaled up our prices over the next five years and scaled up the number of people we taught. We eventually went on to teach 20,000 people a week-long wealth training course at $5,000 per person. Do the math. It's breathtaking.

Then, Saddam Hussein invaded Kuwait. The United States launched Desert Storm on January 17, 1991. People started watching the bombs drop and stopped attending seminars. Our business dried up. It was time to scale things back down to zero. We closed our doors for the next seven years.

When the conditions were right, we started to scale things back up. As a test, Tom Painter and I started a financial tele-coaching business in 1999. Tele-coaching was just in its infancy then. Our first online class had eight people who paid $1,000 for a series of live weekly teleconferences with me. From that small re-beginning, we grew into one of the largest training operations for real estate investment education in the world. Hundreds of thousands of students have attended our one-day to three-day free events. Tens of thousands more became protégés who have paid up to $5,000 to learn more. And several thousand students have graduated from our Mastery Program, which has a tuition of up to $30,000. With our coaching, these students have earned over a billion dollars in actual profits and have donated over $30 million to various charities of their choice.

And from all of this intellectual property, my partners and I have brought in over a billion dollars in gross revenue. That's billion with a "b."

It's taken me over 30 years—and several incarnations—to learn the ins and outs of the information business. I love this business so much that I actually coined the word "Info-Preneur." At times, it can be a very lucrative business. At other times, it can be very, very difficult. Through it all, the scaling up and the down, I keep pursuing my purpose of teaching people how to become enlightened entrepreneurs and info-preneurs.

Recently, I've begun sharing my secrets with selected info-marketers. I show them how to generate their own billions in a program I call Info-Preneuring: How to Be an Information Multi-Millionaire. Do you qualify for such a program?

Do you have a book in you? Or a speech in you? Or a message in you?

Would you like to turn your E.S.P into a fortune? What is your E.S.P?

E. Experience

S. Story

P. Passion

With the right guidance, you can transform what you already know into millions.

So how do you earn your fortune with intellectual property?

I know what it's like to go from bestselling author to bankrupt businessman and back again with over a billion dollars in info-product sales. If you're struggling through bleak financial times, all I can say is, "I totally understand!" I've earned the right to tell you that you can survive and prosper…starting right now with what you already have.

The money can start to flow into your life in as few as 24 hours from this very moment. What?!!! 24 hours from now? Yup. Look at a clock. Log in the time. Your 24 hours start right now.

RICH IN SIX

In 2008 I shot an infomercial entitled *Rich in Six: How to go from a little to a lot in 6 weeks or less.* In doing the research for this product, I did a tele-conference with a group of participants. One of the students was named Linda and one of her skills was painting. She'd been painting for years but had sold few paintings. It was more of a hobby than a profession. I challenged her on a live conference call to "turn professional." Instead of encouraging her to sell her physical paintings, I challenged her to sell her "how-to" expertise on painting. I coached her to create a 16-week painting seminar. She had never done anything like that before. As soon as she heard the idea, she went into a near-panic. The "how" word started to attack her. How will I sell it? How will I deliver it? How can I find people who might want it? How? How? How?

She beat back her uncertainties and put together an email message and sent to about 150 of her friends and family members. I advised her to create scarcity by saying in her email that she had only ONE spot available. She offered a long-distance coaching program for ONE budding art student. Using a telephone, the internet and a networked camera, she reasoned she would be able to teach basic painting skills to anyone. How was she going to hook up a camera? She didn't know. How was she actually going to teach successfully? She didn't know. She just knew that somehow she'd be able to figure it out.

My challenge came to her on a Monday afternoon at about five. She spent the rest of the day wondering and worrying. Then, she found clarity in her mind and heart for exactly what she would do. Twenty-two hours after she had been challenged, she sent the email. It offered to mentor someone to paint in a sixteen-week course for $1,000 tuition, payable immediately.

Exactly two hours later she received the following email:

Hi, Linda.

Are you sure you can teach me to paint over the phone??

If so - I always felt we had a connection ever since we met at that seminar...

I would love to be your 16-week student and I have the $1000!!!

Debra Jo

Following is the email that Linda sent me after she had just made a thousand dollars in a single day from idea to cash.

Hi, Bob

I felt a little shaken up on Monday after the Rich in Six tele- conference. :-) When your mentor tells you exactly what you can do—I figure you'd better do it. So I did—I pushed away any fears and spent the rest of Monday thinking about how I would structure my offer. And Tuesday morning wrote out my email.

I checked and Debra Jo's email is marked as arriving at 5:06 Tuesday. Exactly 24 hours after the call ended the day before!

She and I are both excited! Thank you for your great mentoring!

Linda

She turned her **e**xpertise, **s**tory and **p**assion into $1,000 cash. That may not seem like much to you. But I'd launched my billion dollar train- ing business almost exactly the same way nearly 30 years earlier—an eight-week course on real estate investing for $75.

Let's just dream for a minute. How could Linda turn this simple suc- cess into a million dollar-a-year empire using the Millionaire Matrix? Well, we already know that someone might be willing to invest $1,000 for a 16-week course. How many more people does she need to at- tract? One million dollars is generated from only a thousand students. Do you think there might be another 1,000 people somewhere in the world who might want the same experience? Absolutely!

Here's the problem…she is only one person and she can't teach 1000 people in a one-on-one course. She has to scale things up. Look at the Millionaire Matrix. Maybe she could create an online course for $100 and market it to 10,000 people. Do the math. That's a million, isn't it?

The Millionaire Matrix. Information products can become VERY, VERY exciting VERY, VERY quickly.

THERE'S A BOOK IN YOU!

You also have a book or info-product in you that's worth discovering. When it comes to the information business, your story is the most important story. Writing a book about your experience is your most important product. So you scan through your cache of problems, or fears or failures that have happened in your life. Make a decision to solve or resolve them one by one. Everyone likes a survivor. But everyone LOVES a winner!

That's your richest vein of gold. Your story is easy for you to sell. Why? Because it's true for you. It's comes from your own experience—from your own heart and your own mind. Therefore, as you share your testimony about what happened to you, it's real. It's authentic. It's enlightened selling because you passionately believe in it. It is your lowest-hanging fruit.

If Nicky and Linda and I can do it, so can you.

About Robert

Robert Allen has been teaching ordinary people how to achieve extraordinary success and financial freedom for over 30 years. He is the author of some of the most influential financial books of all time, including the *New York Times* mega-bestsellers "Creating Wealth," "Nothing Down," "Multiple Streams of Income" and the co-author of "The One Minute Millionaire." His most recent book is entitled "Cash in a Flash."

Today there are literally thousands of millionaires who attribute their success to Mr. Allen's systems and strategies. The National Speakers Association has named him "America's Top Millionaire Maker."

He is a popular television and radio guest who appears on hundreds of radio and television programs including "Good Morning America," and Regis Philbin and Larry King's shows. He has been the subject of articles in numerous international publications including the *Wall Street Journal*, the *Los Angeles Times*, the *Washington Post, Newsweek, Barron's, Money* magazine and *Reader's Digest*, to name just a few.

Robert Allen believes it is part of his purpose in life to teach people how to achieve financial success—even starting from nothing. To prove this, he once said:

"Send me to any city. Take away my wallet. Give me $100 for living expenses. And in 72 hours, I'll buy an excellent piece of real estate using none of my own money."

Challenged by the *Los Angeles Times* to live up to his claim, he flew to San Francisco with an reporter from that paper and proceeded to buy six properties within 57 hours. The *L.A. Times* headline proclaimed, "Buying Home Without Cash-Boastful Investor Accepts *Times'* Challenge and Wins."

Most people assume that "it takes money to make money." With the LA Times challenge, Mr. Allen demonstrated once again that the source of true wealth is an internal reservoir of passion, courage and persistence.

True to the title of one of his books, Mr. Allen loves to generate multiple streams of income. What is one of his favorite streams of income these days? In his bestselling book, "Multiple Streams of Income," he demonstrates how anyone can earn a fortune (like he did) by marketing specific "how-to" information. He calls it Info-Preneuring. He is passionate about teaching people how to turn the ideas in their heads into millions of dollars. See www.robertallen.com.

In the past 30 years, through his books, training sessions, seminars and coaching, his affiliated companies have generated over a BILLION dollars in gross revenue. More importantly, his students have generated over a BILLION dollars in NET profits by using his strategies and techniques.

On the home front, Robert and his wife, Daryl, just celebrated 35 years of marriage and are the proud parents of three children: Amae, Aaron and Hunter.

A message from Robert G. Allen about our current economic circumstances:

"I tend to take a long view of our economic circumstances. I try not to get distracted by the short-term fluctuations in the stock market, the price of gasoline, the unemployment statistics and interest rates. Here are some major trends I see which will have a dramatic impact on individuals and societies. None of these trends are surprising. They've been underway for decades.

1) Entrepreneurship is increasing:
This recent financial downturn should have awakened ALL of us to the need to have multiple streams of income. As a result, more people worldwide are making the decision to take control of their own financial destinies. Each family should develop side businesses to supplement their incomes from their jobs.

2) Competition is increasing:
There will be more economic pressure from the emerging economies that are embracing entrepreneurship: Brazil, India, Russia, Mexico and China. There will be more competition, more commerce between countries, more business failures and more fortunes being made by smart business people who handle increased competition with tighter business controls.

3) Instability and volatility is increasing:
We are becoming more interdependent worldwide—and therefore, shocks to one economy will reverberate more widely and be felt by many others. Small businesses will need to make faster decisions. Businesses that don't adapt will be swept away more quickly.

4) Business is speeding up.
The speed of the Internet makes business happen in an instant. People will need to become more tech-savvy in order to survive. Within this next decade, over half of the world's population will have access to the Internet. The pace of new business creation and destruction will accelerate. Vast fortunes will be made by those who can handle the new speed of business."

CHAPTER 2

Converting the Masses: A Proven Formula for Profitable Speaking

By Dave VanHoose

What if I told you that there is a way for you to increase your sales while actually doing less work? Would you be interested in learning how to do this?

I have to tell you that this isn't some new whiz-bang internet strategy, but rather one that the world's best-known authors and info-marketers use to build their empires.

Still interested?

Ok, here it is: speaking.

Not public speaking, but rather speaking for profit. Seriously.

Look, if you've ever given a thought to doing webinars, tele-seminars and presentations, then you owe it to yourself to pay close attention to what I'm about to share with you.

In a moment, I'm going to reveal our proven formula for converting audiences into cash. In fact, we know it to be the most effective way to get new customers (short of selling one-to-one, which is impossible to scale up).

It's important that you understand that what I'm about to share with you isn't a theory, but rather a technique that's been battle-tested in the real world.

This blueprint has been developed from real world experience and over 3000 platform presentations. In fact, this same blueprint helped one company generate over $14 million in sales and a spot (No. 35) on the Inc. 500 list of the fastest-growing private companies in America.

So with that said, let's get on with the show, as they say.

THE 7 FIGURE SPEAKING EMPIRE BLUEPRINT

1. **Grab Their Attention:** Open your talk POWERFULLY with a moving story, emotional video, affecting demonstration, funny joke, or even by asking a question to take control of the crowd right from the start.

2. **Build Rapport:** Before the crowd will listen to your message, you must build a rapport with them throughout your presentation. Telling stories, walking into the crowd, and asking questions are just a few of the most effective ways to do this.

3. **Establish Credibility:** The question the audience is silently asking themselves is, "What makes this person qualified to talk about this subject?" Show them with your accomplishments.

4. **Target a Problem They Have (Or One Don't Know They Have):** This is also known as "turning up the pain." You'll need to bring up a problem that the audience has and then make them aware of it. Great speakers can get the audience to *own the problem.*

5. **Show Them That There Is a Solution:** After turning up the pain, you must offer the crowd a solution. For maximum sales conversion, present your product or service as that pain reliever.

6. **Set Their Expectations:** It's a classic formula: tell them what you're going to tell them, tell them, and then tell them what you've told them. And just as important, you need to let them know what you are here to do: sell them on a product or an idea.

7. **Give Social Proof:** You can talk until you are blue in the face to prove a point or explain a concept, but the majority of people won't believe you. Show them testimonials, checks, bank statements or other elements of proof to get them to believe.

8. **Show the Benefits:** So many speakers think that the way to sell people is to tell the audience about the features of a given product or service. People don't spend their money on features. They buy because of the benefits your product or service brings them—so show what those are.

9. **Make An Irresistible Offer:** Nowadays, you can't simply offer a single product. You'll find that if you want to increase your sales, you must provide additional value through bonuses. Reports, phone calls, audio recordings, software and additional products make great bonuses.

10. **Reverse the Risk & Give Them a Guarantee:** The number-one reason why people don't buy your product or service is because they've been let down in the past. If you truly believe in your product, tell the audience and give them a risk-free guarantee.

11. **Give Them a Deadline/Make It Scarce:** Have you ever noticed how much more you can get done when you have a deadline? The same principle applies when you're getting people to take advantage of what you are offering. Let them know there is scarcity, or a deadline, and that they must take action NOW.

12. **Call to Action:** Most speakers tighten up when it comes time make their offer. You must tell the audience that they

need to take action and how to do it. The simplest way is to ask them, "How many of you would like me to share with you the same system that has made me successful?"

Now that you have the formula, you too can leverage the power of this media to recruit and attract NEW clients!

About Dave

Dave VanHoose of the 7 Figure Speaking Empire is a master platform trainer. Dave's masterful execution of sales presentations is evident in his own success and that of his students. Dave is a mentor and speaker coach to some of the most experienced speakers in the seminar industry. He masterfully takes a seasoned veteran and amplifies his or her platform abilities to new levels. What is Dave's secret? Experience! This top closer has mastered the art of platform persuasion and personally delivered more than 3000 stage presentations.

His leadership and sales abilities took his first seminar-based sales company, Foreclosures Daily, to number 35 on *Inc.* magazine's list of the 500 fastest-growing companies in the U.S. Within three years, Dave's company had 100 employees and over $30 million in revenue, and was producing 50 to 100 seminar events per month!

Dave is a true example of a winning spirit. He attributes his success to his ability to accept nothing less than the best and his commitment to a mindset of abundance. It is this same focus on excellence that allowed him to play a critical team role during the 2003 Tampa Bay Storm ArenaBowl (XVII) world championship season! His insistence on a strong mental and physical commitment has provided him with the ability to overcome the many obstacles he has faced in his life, including complete paralysis at the age of 29. His ability to inspire leadership and provide speakers with the tools and strategies they need continually raises the caliber of speakers throughout the industry.

Dave has focused his business life on motivating world-class people to achieve more than they ever thought possible. His own achievements have led him to channel his success and energy into his new charitable foundation.

In his spare time, Dave enjoys spending time with the ladies in his life: his lovely wife and daughter.

Dave is available for a limited number of speaking engagements, tele-seminars and interviews. To inquire about Dave's availability, call 800-687-4061 and ask for Nicole.

To claim your FREE GIFT, be sure to visit http://www.SpeakingEmpire.com too, and pick up a copy of Dave's Proven, Powerful & Profitable Presentation Formula (valued at $197).

CHAPTER 3

The New Rules for Attracting Quality Clients: High-Touch, High-Experience Strategies

By Dustin Mathews

Sometimes, you don't need a huge amount of money or effort to make the sale.

Sometimes, you just need to be a little creative.

And sometimes...it just takes a little pepperoni.

One of our clients, Russell, was trying to contact somebody who he really wanted to team up with for a joint venture. He was trying and trying to get his foot in the door and nothing was working—not email, not snail mail, not phone calls, *nothing*.

He was very frustrated, as this was a deal he really wanted and needed to make. And he couldn't just head over to this man's office and knock on the door—Russell was in Utah and the executive he wanted to contact was in downtown Manhattan.

But Russell wasn't ready to give up—and he finally brainstormed a brilliant idea that might finally do the trick. Around lunchtime in New York, Russell jumped on the Internet and found a well-reviewed pizza place located right around the corner from the exec's office. So he called the pizza place, ordered a delivery to go to the office, and included a twenty-dollar tip—if the pizza place would do him a big favor.

The favor?

They had to deliver the pizza with a note taped to the top of the box reading, "Hey, it's Russell. Have lunch on me. I've been trying to get in touch with you and I think we could do business together. Give me a call."

Russell's phone number was, of course, at the bottom of the note.

Well, within ten minutes of the delivery, the guy called him. And the result? They began doing business together and generated hundreds of thousands of dollars with their new joint venture.

And it only took 30 minutes or less.

CREATING SHOCK AND AWE

In the story I just told you, Russell jump-started an incredibly profitable relationship with someone he hardly knew at all—and he did it for under $50.

He managed to do this because he did something unique and out-of-the-box—and he also provided what we call at our company, 7 Figure Speaking Empire, "high-touch, high-experience." Russell dreamed up incredible fantastic way to make a memorable connection—triggering a pizza delivery from the other side of the country.

A "high-touch, high-experience" strategy is one of the hallmarks of what we consider the new rules of marketing and sales. Since the recession a few years ago, there's no question that economic conditions have improved. People are willing to spend money again. But, for most, budgets are still a lot tighter than they were before 2008. That's why it's critical to get people revved up about what you're selling in exciting new ways.

This is something we put into practice in our company every single day.

And, as an introduction to our approach to this thinking, I'd like to say that we understand all the firepower that automation, gadgets and online information marketing techniques can bring to the party these days. And we like what the digital world has to offer. But at the moment, everyone else is using these electronic avenues as their primary marketing delivery method—which makes it harder and harder for your sales messages to stand out from the herd.

Something is lost in all that—call it "the personal touch," or whatever you'd like. But as Russell will tell you, though the best-crafted email in the world might not make an impression, a hand-delivered pizza definitely will.

On a more practical level, relying solely on digital modes of communication also introduces another danger—that the message never even *reaches* the recipient. To get to the really important people, the decision-makers who determine whether you get a certain piece of business or not, you invariably have to get past their gatekeepers *first*.

Secretaries, personal assistants and even virtual assistants are screening calls and emails and determining what's of value and what's not before passing anything on to their demanding superiors. Most of them really can't know if an unsolicited marketing message is worthy of their boss's time, so they just erase the voicemail or drop the email in the trash folder, rather than risk getting reprimanded for forwarding on junk mail.

That's why it's important, and even *essential*, to develop other high-impact methods to make the kind of connection you're seeking. And that's why we dedicate ourselves to that approach.

OUR HIGH-TOUCH, HIGH-EXPERIENCE SECRETS

One of the major services that we offer is what we call a "Power Day." When a client books a Power Day, they come to see us personally for help so they can leave with the most effective way to sell their product or service. We actually write out the optimum sales presentation for their product or service, and then we teach the client how to deliver that message, so that when they leave, they're ready for success.

We've done over 3000 presentations ourselves, so we've developed a proven formula that's been put to the test over and over again. It's great to be able to pass on these secrets to our clients. In some instances, we've helped them boost their revenues by six- or seven-figure numbers by giving them the key to generating repeatable successful sales.

Of course, just as in any other business, we need to bring in new clients of our own so that we can continue to grow. In order to do that, we have to sell our own value to them first. This is where our "high-touch, high-experience" marketing comes into play—it's specially crafted to help us stand out from the pack and establish our selling credentials. The fact is, how can a client trust us to help him or her sell things if we can't sell ourselves?

Our marketing process starts immediately after we get a lead, so that we can jump-start the kind of high experience we're after. The first thing we do is ship them a "Shock and Awe" package via Federal Express for overnight delivery. It's not as tasty as a pizza, but it does deliver a ton of credibility.

That's because our "Shock and Awe" box contains a tremendous amount of our material in a variety of media formats—binders, books, DVDs and other informational products. This demonstrates our expertise immediately; if we've written best-selling books and produced professional videos, obviously we are operating at a high level ourselves. Few other sales gurus can fill up this kind of package the way we can—and our leads, who are invariably serious players, know that.

If our "Shock and Awe" package doesn't get an initial response, we don't stop there. About once every week or so for the next ten weeks, our lead will get something in the mail from us that's designed to be an entertaining surprise, such as a box of cookies with a little note that reads, "Sweet things happen when you work with Speaking Empire."

Or we'll go down to the bank, get five brand-new crisp dollar bills, staple them to a piece of paper, and send it out with a note on it saying, "We look forward to making money together with you."

We don't use any used car salesman tactics or high-pressure sales pitches. Instead, we employ cute and fun techniques that other people just don't or won't do. What's more likely to get someone's attention: an email with a desperate subject heading in all caps, or a box of cookies delivered to his or her office? There's nothing like getting a package in the mail. It brings with it a positive and tangible feeling that can't be replicated through digital communications, especially since we make sure to put something *good* in these packages—whether it's a sweet treat like the cookies or just cold, hard cash!

These packages are usually the best way to bypass the gatekeepers I spoke about earlier in this chapter. Direct mailings are also a lot more effective than calls or emails. One of the big reasons for this is that people don't use snail mail for much anymore. We stand out in a memorable way: Rather than inducing a cringe from yet another hard marketing push (the kind we all have to endure on a daily basis), we make our target smile.

ADDING ENERGY TO OUR POWER DAYS

When we do sign up a lead for one of our Power Days, we continue to apply our high-touch, high-experience techniques to make sure he or she feels that he or she is getting first-class treatment from us. That starts with something they're totally not expecting—we send a limo to pick them up at the start of the day.

Right away, that limo sets the tone for the consulting day and gets our lead in a great mood. We engineer the rest of the day to be equally relaxing, even though we get a lot of work done. Our lead meets with us and our team at our office here in Tampa, Florida. Later, we have a nice relaxing lunch right on the water at a top restaurant. As the day progresses, we have breaks built in so that the lead can unwind, and, by the end of the day, he or she leaves with an awesome sales pitch that's hand-tailored to him or her and his or her business. We also take a picture with our lead while he or she is with us and blast it out through all the big social media channels, to give the lead and his or her business some extra unsolicited promotion across our large professional network.

Since we work so hard to make the experience with us so outstanding, we almost always get a testimonial from our lead at the end of the day—and we also end up getting many solid referrals. Even after the Power Day is over, we continue to follow up by sending the lead our newsletter (again through the regular mail). Yes, a digital newsletter would be a lot easier and cheaper, but we're not after easy and cheap. We're committed to a high-touch, high- experience business model.

This is why we *also* send the lead the photo we took on the Power Day. No, it's not a JPEG file, it's an actual 8 x 10 photo, professionally framed and accompanied by a handwritten thank-you note. In yet *another* mailing, we send the lead an oversized poster based on what he or she learned with us.

Now, you might ask, why do all this? We've already provided the service that was contracted—why go to the hassle and expense of creating all these other benefits? The truth is that we work with very high-end clients, and we're willing to reinvest the money we've made into making them feel as special as possible. Not only does this kind of high-touch, high-experience marketing keep them feeling good about working with Speaking Empire, but it also stimulates great word-of-mouth buzz for us.

At the end of the day, it may be a little more trouble and a little more work for us— but it gives our reputation and our image *more* than a little boost in the eyes of the outside world.

SPENDING MONEY TO MAKE MONEY

What it all comes down to is this: If you want a client to invest in *you*, you have to also invest in *him*. High-touch, high-experience techniques are an awesome way to demonstrate that investment—they also boost conversions, create referrals and differentiate your marketing from that of the competition in a meaningful way.

I opened this chapter with my friend Russell's brilliant "high-touch" pizza strategy. I'd like to close with a more expensive high-tech and high-touch case study, courtesy of another our clients, Walter Bergeron, who's the president of Power Control Services in Louisiana.

Walter had the same kind of problem as Russell had—he couldn't get to the company decision-makers in order to make a sale. The difference was that he wasn't trying to reach some high-level executive. No, he had a highly technical product that required the recommendation of a firm's *engineers* before the higher-ups would even consider buying it.

You might think it would be easier to get to the engineers than to the top managers, but you'd be wrong—it was a *lot harder* for Walter to do. Executives were more accustomed to being sold to and able to identify might be valuable to their businesses, but engineers weren't receptive to marketing at all. And it proved impossible to get past *their* "gatekeepers" in order to demonstrate the value of Walter's product.

So Walter took this idea and executed it like gangbusters. It was, however, going to cost a bit more than a pizza—more like $200 per client for this particular "high-touch" strategy.

This idea called for the creation of a special device, housed in an industrial case, that contained many of our recommended "Shock and Awe" box components—printed information about Walter, his company and the product in question. But all that information was buried under the real attraction—the one that was actually going to generate the desired "Shock and Awe," as far as the engineers were concerned.

When they opened the case, they experienced James Bond moments—because digital video screens popped up automatically into their lines of sight. In front of each screen was a button with a note that said, "Push me." When the recipient went ahead and pressed the button, a seven-minute video played that demonstrated the product and *showed* what it was all about. The case was specially designed to be shipped anywhere without damage to the video mechanism.

As I said, each device cost around $200. Walter sent out eight of them.

And he generated over $30,000 in sales from that $1600 investment.

So sometimes it only takes a pizza…and sometimes it takes a really cool device that's like something you'd see in a Hollywood blockbuster. But find out whatever it *does* take, and put it into play so that you can grab the attention of the person you're after and start a mutually beneficial relationship.

High-touch, high-experience techniques lead to high-powered results. Reach high, and your sales will follow.

Would you like to experience your very own Power Day and join the insiders' club for thought leaders, centers of influence and the world's leading communicators? Simply visit www.SpeakingEmpire.com or call us at 800-687-4061 to see if you qualify.

About Dustin

Dustin Mathews' expertise in Internet marketing has earned him national accolades and the respect of the information marketing industry. He publishes the most widely-read offline newsletter for speakers, affiliates and promoters. This Internet marketing guru started his entrepreneurial path as the marketing genius behind the success of Foreclosures Daily. His expertise was critical to helping take that business to the No. 35 position on the Inc. 500 list of the fastest-growing companies in the U.S. During his time at FD, Dustin managed and marketed more than 200 events per month and generated over $14 million in sales. Dustin quickly became known for his abilities to create marketing frenzies which drive people to buy millions in products and services, both online and offline.

After his success at FD, Dustin founded Business Credit Infusion™. As the company's Chief Marketing Officer, he empowers business owners and entrepreneurs to get the money they need for their businesses.

Today, his success in generating over $11 million in online sales for clients launching products has made him one of the most highly sought-after product launch experts. However, most of his time these days is spent educating industry experts on the specialized processes he has developed. His mentoring services are a core component of the success of the 7 Figure Speaking Empire.

What's next for this Florida State University graduate? Dustin is now focused on championing a new business called The Internet Movement, which will concentrate on leveraging traditional public relations methods to procure new clients for the information marketing industry. The intent is to catalyze new organic growth for the industry as a whole. Dustin is committed to sharing his insights and successes with a wider audience, so that more people will become impassioned to achieve higher levels of success.

Dustin is the co-author of "How to Get Rich Working For FREE," "Online Marketing Secrets Revealed" and "Secrets of the Real Estate Millionaires." In his downtime, Dustin enjoys playing tennis and mountain biking with his wife Missy.

CHAPTER 4

How to Profit From The Real Estate Meltdown

By Sherman Ragland, CCIM

In this chapter, I'm going to tell you what really happened to the American housing and mortgage markets, show you who's benefiting in the aftermath, and explain how you can, too!

WHAT HAPPENED?

When I was a kid, my dad would say, "There are three types of people in this world: those who make things happen, those who watch things happen, and those who say, 'Hey, what just happened?'" Right now, it seems like a lot of folks are in the third category, asking, "What the heck happened to my job, my retirement account, and the value of my home?"

In July 2007, before a packed audience of 450 at our local real estate investor club meeting, I predicted the collapse of the U.S. stock market and housing market, Countrywide's bankruptcy, and the possible beginning of the next Great Depression. The last of these did not come to pass, but what we went through was pretty scary.

Was I psychic?

No, I was simply an active real estate investor who was paying attention and didn't like what I was seeing.

I remembered going to a settlement about eight months earlier in which we were selling a property we'd rehabbed in downtown Baltimore. As the sellers, we walked out of the settlement with a fat check. But it was the buyer's "take" that gave me pause.

The buyer, a first-time homeowner with sketchy credit, not only got the keys to the home, but drove to it in his brand-new BMW and picked up a check for nearly $10,000. He'd been able to secure a loan for 110% of the purchase price of the property—so he received $155,000 to purchase a $145,000 home and had enough left to go shopping for a plasma TV.

I walked out of there thinking, "The mortgage market is about to crash and burn." I was off by about eight months, but by June 2007, word on the street was that 90% of the subprime mortgages originated that year were already in default.

The seeds for the subprime meltdown were sown years earlier in the fall of 1987, when the U.S. housing market had been through its worst bubble in over 50 years. The principal reason was the deregulation of the financial markets during the early 1980s, which led to huge amounts of new money flowing into real estate and a crazy tax policy that allowed people to invest a dollar in real estate and get seven dollars' worth of tax write-offs. This tax legislation was changed in 1986; within a year, the money flowing into real estate was cut off.

Within three years, every city in America had a glut of real estate projects, from single-family houses to golf courses to empty office buildings. Unfortunately the contemporaneous collapse of the real estate market brought about a wave of foreclosures, and in its wake the collapse of savings and loan associations all over America.

The government created the Resolution Trust Corporation, or RTC, to deal with this multi-billion dollar problem. Whenever there's a massive problem involving money, Wall Street is sure to come up with a solution, and the grand one they created was SECURITIZATION. Wall Street would buy the bad real estate loans and real estate from the government for pennies on the dollar, and then hire workout specialists who would go back to the borrowers and offer to restructure the loans so the borrowers could get back to paying something. If the borrower could not come to terms, then the specialist would be given permission to foreclose on the property and sell the real estate to recover the money.

The pooling of loans, followed by selling shares of the combined pools to institutional investors, worked like a charm, and suddenly the multi-billion dollar problem that was projected to take 20 to 30 years to fix was solved in 10. By 1998, the RTC was no longer around, but Wall Street had invested heavily in the infrastructure necessary to create real estate securities on a massive scale. And so in the late 1990s, the subprime mortgage was born.

The very same group of people who came together to clean up one big mess soon created a new product that would lead to the biggest financial meltdown in U.S. history.

Soon after Wall Street created the subprime loans, it developed other types of loan products for borrowers who would never qualify for traditional mortgages; these products were known by the mortgage professionals who sold them as "liar loans."

By the summer of 2007, Wall Street, in partnership with companies like Countrywide, had sold trillions of dollars of these toxic loans to investors and financed trillions of dollars of real estate to these questionable borrowers.

But by spring 2007, the chickens had started coming home to roost. In April 2007, the industry's first-quarter report revealed that 90% of the sub-prime loans issued in the first quarter of 2007 were in default.

Eighteen months later, the subprime market had totally collapsed, the entire mortgage industry was in trouble, and it had become clear that these toxic loans had seeped into the investment portfolios of hundreds of thousands of banks, insurance companies and state retirement funds. By September of 2008, the entire U.S. economy came to a screeching halt.

WHY YOU SHOULD CARE

It's only by taking a little time to understand what happened do you stand a real chance of benefiting from it.

Imagine that you and your spouse and kids take a three-week summer vacation each year at a certain mountain resort with a pool. One year, you arrive there and are told, "Unfortunately, the water drained out of the pool last night, and we're not sure why."

After a couple of days without water in the pool, several other families who are only taking a ten-day vacation leave the resort to find a spot with a working pool, because they can't "waste" their entire vacation waiting for the pool to get fixed. But for you and your family, who have 21 days to relax, it's a smaller inconvenience, and you decide to hang around. In fact, the prospect of almost having the pool to yourselves once it's fixed is very appealing.

Why should you to risk it? Because the resort has assured you that there is nothing fundamentally wrong with the pool. While you wait for them to refill it, you can enjoy the other activities the resort has to offer

If you had been told that the pool would be closed for the summer for repairs, you would have made other travel plans. But in this case, the pool will be fine.

Some people are making money right now in real estate while others are too scared to go back in the water.

There is nothing fundamentally wrong with real estate, but the supply of money used to finance it was severely over-inflated for a number of years and then disappeared overnight. But unlike the resort, we know what happened to the "water." It left real estate like a herd of stampeding cattle, out of the barn, over the hill, and into anything, and everything, EXCEPT mortgages to finance single-family homes.

So why do I say there is nothing wrong with real estate?

Unlike the real estate bubble of the late 1980s, this so-called "housing bubble" was really created in reaction to the increase in "liar loans" from 1996 to 2007. And it was the crises that originated in the mortgage market starting in the spring of 2007 that ultimately brought about the financial meltdown and the resulting recession.

SO, WHAT'S NEXT?

The smart money is already buying up real estate.

Warren Buffett, the second-wealthiest person in America, said recently on CNBC's "Squawk Box," "If I had a way of buying a couple hundred thousand single-family homes...I would load up on them."

Peter Lynch, probably the most respected mutual fund money manager of all time, ran the Fidelity Magellan Fund from 1977 to 1990, during which time it went from a $18 million fund to an $18 billion one. Lynch wrote in his bestselling book on stock market investing, "One Up On Wall Street," "Before you do invest anything in stocks, you ought to consider buying a house, since a house, after all, is the one good investment almost everyone manages to make...in 99 cases out of 100, a house will be a money-maker."

But it's not just Buffett and Lynch who are buying real estate; if you look at the S.& P./Case-Shiller home price indices, you see that over the past two years the number of cash buyers has been increasing steadily.

When you see the phrase "cash buyer," you should think, "Real Estate INVESTOR!" A "cash buyer" is not someone who paid 100% cash for a property; rather, it is someone who DID NOT use a loan that was later sold to Fannie Mae, Freddie Mac or the Federal Housing Administration. In other words, a cash buyer is an investor, and in almost every city in America, they now make up 50% to 80% of the market.

WHY REAL ESTATE?

The reason why real estate investors are jumping into the housing market in droves is that in most markets housing prices are so low that for the first time in almost seven years, single-family houses will automatically generate a positive cash flow as soon as they are purchased, fixed up, and rented out.

As the dean of the nation's only dedicated school of real estate investing, I have often written that real estate is the **IDEAL** investment.

When you compare real estate to the other major investment choices, like stocks, bonds, mutual funds, forex, gold, oil and gas, collectible art, wine, or antiques, there is no question that it has a number of key advantages. And right now, they're especially compelling.

Specifically, there are five key things that real estate offers versus any other investment:

I – Income: Every investment goes up and down in value, but not every investment provides income on an ongoing basis. Even when real estate goes down in value on paper, this decrease can have little to no impact on actual income. In fact, the monthly income from a rental property is not usually tied to the property's value. And many investors who have been told that their property value had decreased have actually seen their incomes rise from their rental properties. Some even petition their local municipalities or counties to have their property taxes reduced because of the losses in paper value, and in doing so, actually increased their income streams!

D – Depreciation (or tax shelter): Another way in which real estate is unique is that while other investments typically have no tax benefits, the government actually allows property owners to shelter some of their income from taxes by allowing owners of rental properties the opportunity to depreciate their properties over several years. The depreciation amount acts as an offset to the taxes due. Diane Kennedy, CPA and author of "Loopholes of the Rich" has described real estate as the "last great legal tax shelter."

E – Equity Building: By far the least understood and single greatest benefit of owning income-producing real estate, equity building can also be described as "forced savings" for homeowners and conservative-minded real estate investors. When you acquire a property, you usually choose between an amortizing and a non-amortizing loan. Most amortizing loans are available in the United States for a term of 15 or 30 years. Each month that an amortizing loan is in place, the borrower makes a single payment, but a portion of it is applied to BOTH the interest charged by the lender AND the principal amount the lender provided. At the end of the term of an amortizing loan, the ENTIRE loan amount is paid off. If you acquire a million-dollar property and use a 15-year amortizing loan, you will own that property free and clear at the end. Even if the property does not increase in value, you still have an asset that is worth at least $1 million. If the property in question is not your own home, but rather a small apartment house, and every dollar you collect goes towards running the property and paying off your 15-year amortizing mortgage, you're breaking even but get richer by paying off the mortgage. At the end of 15 years, you essentially got a bunch of people together to give you a million dollars, assuming the property did not go up or down in value during that period. How long would it take you save a million after-tax dollars? The same forced saving effect occurs when you own your own home, use an amortizing mortgage, and REFUSE to use a home equity loan. Equity building is by far the most overlooked yet most powerful advantage of real estate investing.

A – Appreciation: Everyone is familiar with the advice "buy low and sell high." Real estate markets across the country have taken such a beating that values are often as low as they have been in a decade. In many markets, they've already reached bottom. If history repeats itself, once real estate starts heading up, it will continue in that direction for a long time.

L – Leverage: To buy $100,000 worth of stocks, you typically need $100,000; to buy $100,000 worth of gold, you need $100,000. BUT to acquire $100,000 dollars worth of real estate, you typically need only $20,000. If you're an investor with good credit, you can acquire an income-producing property for 20% of its value, and if you're already a homeowner, then most lenders will accept 10%. If you have good credit and are a savvy real estate investor, or as we say, a REALINVESTOR®, you know how to acquire a $100,000 property for much less than $20,000, regardless of your FICO score. If you buy a $100,000 property, get a 20% rate of return over five years, and then sell it, you'll make $120,000. After you pay off the $80,000 loan, you've made $20,000 on a $20,000 investment, a 100% return on in 5 years.

Together, these five unique attributes (**I = Income, D = Depreciation, E = Equity Buildup, A = Appreciation, L = Leverage**) make real estate the **IDEAL** investment.

HERE'S HOW YOU CAN MAKE MONEY IN REAL ESTATE!

So, while other people are taking advantage of the real estate recovery taking place across the country, it's time for you to answer the question, "How am I going to make money off this?"

Although the late-night TV gurus would like you to believe that there are over 1001 ways to buy real estate, the reality is that there are only 12 fundamental ways to put together a real estate deal, and the combination of these 12 create a variety of opportunities. In a handful of states, including my state of Maryland, there are some specific laws regarding homeowners in foreclosure. Because of these unique laws, there is a 13th totally unique strategy called "Foreclosure Consulting" for those people who live in states with laws such as the Maryland Protection of Homeowners in Foreclosure Act, or PHFA.

These 13 fundamental strategies can be lumped into three categories: **"Quick Cash," "Nothing Down"** and **"Wealth Building"** strategies.

Right now, significant numbers of experienced real estate investors are taking advantage of low prices to build portfolios of properties with a positive cash flow. The real opportunity for new investors is in helping these more experienced investors and in doing so, "getting paid to learn" the business. These are "quick cash" strategies; the two primary ones are "bird dogging" and wholesaling, which can you learn in a weekend. In most cases, you don't need a license or prior experience to get involved; all you need is to find these experienced investors.

To claim your FREE Gift, please visit www.HowToProfitFromTheMeltdown.com.

About Sherman

For the past 12 years, I have served as the Dean of the Realinvestors Academy, which I founded just outside Washington, D.C.

The Realinvestors Academy is the nation's only full-time training program with licensed professional staff dedicated to teaching adults how to become professional real estate investors on either a part-time or full-time basis. We also host online training programs that are viewed around the world.

Prior to founding the Realinvestors Academy, I was involved in over $1.2 billion worth of real estate projects, including representing the federal government in the sale of over $500 million in real estate assets as an RTC and FDIC Asset Disposition Contractor, and the D.C. government in the sale of the land for the Newseum. I also worked for D.C.-based developers responsible for developing over 3,000 acres of land and three office buildings.

More importantly, I have been personally involved in over $30 million in real estate projects in the greater D.C. region, and in the process earned the coveted CCIM designation from the Certified Commercial Institute of the National Association of Realtors. In 2001, I had the pleasure of co-founding the Greater Washington, D.C. Real Estate Investors' Association (http://dcreia.com); it has grown into the largest active real estate investors' group on the East Coast.

CHAPTER 5

The Proven Principles of Success that Turn your J-O-B into your J-O-Y

By Dave VanHoose

There are proven principles of success and if you follow them, you can win at anything you put your mind to. This is true, no matter where you're from, what your background is, or even what your intelligence level is.

One of the first principles of success is to find out what you truly love to do and what ignites your passion.

I believe that each and every one of us was born with a special gift, something we're naturally good at and therefore enjoy and have fun doing.

I talk about this in my new book, "Winning Now: Turning Your J-O-B into your J-O-Y and Never Work Again."

Up to 95 percent of people work in a J-O-B in which they are unhappy, and thus spend the majority of their lives doing something that makes them miserable.

Why would anyone want to do this? Especially when they don't have to?

Crack the code by asking yourself, "What is my natural ability and natural skill?" and things will start to change for the better. Your J-O-B becomes your J-O-Y once you get involved in something that you love and at which you naturally excel.

THE FLOW OF MONEY

Through working with thousands of people, I've found that most don't focus first on learning what they're naturally good or what brings them joy.

Instead, their first thoughts are, "I want to make money, I want to make money. I need to make money."

This isn't a good approach, because something happens when your focus is solely on money, or rather your lack of money. You don't get money!

But when you put your focus on what you love to do and what you are willing to do, the money will show up. It's almost like magic.

This is how it works: the universe requires you to build value before you can get value back. In other words, you can't get something for nothing. When you're doing the things you love, you're building value. This is what attracts money to you.

CHALLENGES AREN'T OBSTACLES,
BUT OPPORTUNITIES

Fortunately, for me–and I am choosing to use the word "fortunately"– I've faced a lot of challenges.

I grew up in middle America in a middle-class family. My parents divorced, which meant I was from a broken family. I also had a learning disability called dyslexia, which makes it harder to learn how to read.

By the time I reached my late twenties, I had problems that affected my health and well-being. At 29, I had a seriously bad back. I had surgery for this, but the operation nearly left me paralyzed. Just a year later, when I was only 30, an eye disease ruined my sight.

In my career, I became very successful by creating a business from the ground up, and through a lot of hard work, building it into a multimillion-dollar company. But later on, circumstances forced me to leave that company and I then had to file for bankruptcy. I nearly lost everything.

All of these things could have short-circuited my success or made me give up, if I had let them.

But the reality is that these challenges came with valuable lessons. Each one of them taught me about what I needed to do to move forward. Instead of holding me back, they ultimately helped me find more success.

I've worked with many multimillionaires, business owners and successful entrepreneurs. One trait I've found that they have in common is an amazing talent for perseverance. When they experience a challenge, they don't give up. They continue to press forward, to improve and to learn.

That's what true winners do.

It's inevitable that you're going to get knocked down. You can't have success without experiencing a lot of failures.

It's like you're going to be in a boxing ring, get punched in the nose and fall down. My question is, are you going to be the person who stays on the mat? Or are you going to get back up, learn from your mistakes and move on?

Winners have the attitude that they aren't going to give up. They persevere when facing difficulties and learn from their failures.

TWO "SHORTCUTS" TO SUCCESS

When people ask me if there are any shortcuts to success, I always say, "absolutely."

When you have to figure out everything yourself through trial and error, you'll be taking the long way.

To find shortcuts, model yourself on successful people and/or hire a mentor or coach.

Modeling yourself on successful people involves learning what has worked for them and then recreating those behaviors or strategies.

The mentors and coaches you can hire have been where you want to go. From their own experience and knowledge, they can give you systems and tools to fast-track your success.

So why not model a successful person or learn from a mentor or coach?

THE NO. 1 MISTAKE AND HOW TO AVOID IT

The first step to success is finding out what your natural talents are. But on the flip side, ignoring your weaknesses will be a big mistake.

So you need to uncover what you're not good at, because successful people know that they can't do everything.

It's a simple truth to remember. You can't be and do everything. You can't be the sales person, the marketing person, the manager, the CFO, and the vice president.

Successful people find out what they're not good at and then use teams and systems to overcome those weaknesses.

We're only as successful as our strongest weaknesses. Leveraging people and systems when needed is definitely a key to success.

PLAY BIG OR DON'T PLAY AT ALL

When I was a young boy, my grandfather would always say to me, "Sonny boy, if you're going to do something, play big or don't play at all."

He was right. If you're going to do something in life, whether it's starting your own business or competing in the Olympics, put your all into it or don't play at all.

This is one of principles that I live by, and one that I teach and coach when working with so many successful entrepreneurs.

Play to win or don't play at all. That attitude right there is going to make sure that you're successful.

But another thing I want you to think about is what success means for you.

Success is different for everyone. For some people, success might be money. For others, it may be winning a world championship. For my wife, success is being a stay-at-home mom.

So first you've got to clarify what is success for you. I believe that a clear description of success is doing what you love to do. This is why I refer to turning your J-O-B into J-O-Y.

The key is to find out what gives you the most happiness and joy, whether you want to be the best mom to your children, start a business, or become a professional athlete or a rock star.

Once you figure that out, you're going to be naturally motivated. You're not going to have to push and swim upstream. You're going to be able to swim downstream because you have found what you love to do.

Some people call it being inspired. I found what I love to do, and I'm completely inspired and have enthusiasm and energy because do what I love.

It's absolutely true. You can turn your J-O-B into your J-O-Y.

CHAPTER 6

The New Rules of Social Media: Link In to Business Success

By Nathan Kievman

It was the most transformational moment in my life...and all I had to do to reach it was break my neck.

When I was sixteen years old, I was in a car accident, which completely knocked me out (and yes, took out a couple of vertebrae). I was unconscious when I was taken to the hospital. And then I woke up. . .

They say you don't really know how many friends you have until you're in trouble. And I was amazed to wake up to *hundreds* of them. High school classmates, teachers, coaches—they were all there, waiting to make sure I was going to be okay.

It was a powerful moment—and it made me realize how strong and how numerous the connections I had made as a teenager were. I really felt like I was part of something bigger than myself—and this experience made a profound difference in my life.

Little did I know then that relationships would become a primary path to my business success—*and* that of my clients.

GETTING "LINKEDIN"

Flash forward to 2008. Like many others during that turbulent year, I was shifting my line of work from real estate investing to business consulting and had attended an event hosted by the marketing guru Jay Abraham. At that event his COO, Spike Humer, mentioned that everyone should be networking on the professional social media site, LinkedIn.

Well, when I got home, I checked it out—and saw that its slogan was, "Relationships Matter." That, of course, resonated with me. So I signed up on the site—and to be honest, I didn't do too much with it for six or seven months. Gradually, however, I found myself using it more and more for a variety of purposes.

The real turning point came when one of my clients asked me what the best way was to recruit a notable list of names for an advisory board for her business. I thought about it, and found that my mind kept going back to the LinkedIn site. I knew there was an amazing collection of professionals who were registered on the site; maybe that network would provide the solution my client was seeking.

So I started identifying the kind of high-level business professionals my client would like to have on her board, and I then began inviting some of them to participate. I started with the very best, figuring I'd have to work my way down to find people who would actually accept the challenge.

Well, lo and behold, my client ended up with an all-star advisory board. I couldn't believe the level of people who had accepted my invitations. That's not a knock against my client—it's just that these were high-caliber people who I just didn't think would be interested. They were people with whom it would have taken my client a long while to connect, and they brought a lot of good opportunities for her business with them.

Since this methodology had paid off so well for this client, I repeated the process for a few more clients, with the same amazing results.

It continued to pay off for me. I reconnected with Larry, one of the speakers from that Jay Abraham event I'd attended almost a year earlier. Larry was building a course on thought leadership marketing. At that event, we'd talked about working together, but then I lost track of him afterwards. Guess where I found him again? LinkedIn, of course.

Anyway, what Larry wanted me to do was promote his webinars so he could get people interested in his new online marketing program. Again, I turned to my new best friend, LinkedIn, and we were able to get hundreds of viewers for that first webinar, which resulted in revenues of more than $30,000 from our first several webinars.

Wow, I thought to myself. LinkedIn was not just about connections. It could also be about *profits*.

I kept promoting Larry's webinars and we continued to add more people to his marketing list. Finally, Larry was invited to speak at a John Assaraf event in San Diego, entitled "Mind, Money and Millions." And it was at this event that I realized that I needed to begin focusing and building my business.

It was time to hone in on my direction.

LOCKING IN A NEW COURSE

I began by taking myself through a process Larry suggested, one that anyone in my position should consider when they're trying to determine the best career path for themselves.

I drew three circles. In one circle, I wrote down the things I really loved to do. In the second, I wrote the things I was really good at. And in the third circle, I wrote what the current trends in the marketplace were.

Then, I turned those circles into something called a Venn Diagram, as in the illustration below:

The areas that those circles have in common—where they over-lapped—would show me where I should focus in terms of business.

What did I love to do? I loved to make relationships happen in the business setting. What was I good at? Creating those relationships for other people. What was a hot trend in the market that would allow me to leverage both my skills and my passion for creating relationships?

Social media.

That was where it all came together for me. I decided to become a social media strategist. And, at the event where I decided on this path, I introduced myself to everyone as if I were already a social media strategist.

I walked out of that event with fifty-six business cards from people who were interested in my services. At the time, nobody else knew how to do social media, but I knew a little more than they did, so that made me the expert.

Now, however, it was time to take it to a whole new level. I made it my mission to figure out all the different ways you could make social media work for a business.

LEARNING THE NEW RULES OF SOCIAL MEDIA

The first thing I was careful about was making sure I could find **practical and systematic approaches** within social media to build business growth. My clients wanted results, but many social media experts were only delivering fluff. Many large corporations might be satisfied with reaching a certain number of Facebook "likes" and "fans," or getting a million Twitter followers, but I didn't see those as true metrics of success—and my clients wouldn't either.

What I did know was that influence boosted the bottom line—so I built up a robust model that enabled social media to become an extension of a business in such a way that it empowered the kind of positive outcomes we all wanted.

I determined there were three elements to the new rules of the game, as they pertained to social media:

- **Trust**
- **Credibility**
- **Elimination of Risk**

In any content we posted, in any transmission we made, in any social media profile we set up and optimized, on whatever platform or site, we had to engage with and focus on these three areas; otherwise, customers would never be completely comfortable doing business with us.

People make buying decisions based on trust; credibility is built through trust; and finally, when you eliminate risk, you enable buying decisions to be made. All three of these elements have a natural interplay with one another.

What this meant was that the old school full-on sales pitch wasn't going to play in a social media world—it would come across as just *not authentic*. Instead, engagement had to be on a one-to-one level. It was micro-marketing, as opposed to mass marketing—but the weird thing was, it was micro-marketing that had to be done on *a mass level*.

How could we pull that off?

Well, I like to say that what I do is *scale personal communication*. Now, some people do that with email and are good at it. But we all receive these very polished html emails with embedded pictures that appear to be the product of very professional marketing, rather than anything authentic.

In contrast, if we pushed authenticity, we pushed your social capital—which, in turn, created trust in your social media connections. And, as business expert Stephen R. Covey conveys in all of his work, *trust is an accelerator of revenue for any organization*.

Now, this approach is much more difficult for bigger brands. They do massive media buys and lots of high-profile advertising, but they don't get in at a smaller intimate level. That's exactly why social media offers such a huge opportunity for small businesses and entrepreneurs. They can take market share away from the bigger companies because they can easily reach customers and clients at the social media level and build on those three elements—trust, credibility and elimination of risk.

To be sure, a lot of smaller organizations still want to use old sales models to enhance their revenues. That's fine, but it's just not going to work in the world of social media. Some also just want to do Facebook or Twitter or Google Plus and ignore the other social media platforms—and you can't do that any longer either.

It's necessary to be active on all the major social media sites and to ensure the same activity isn't cutting across different ones.

What do I mean by that? Many people have software that allows a tweet to be posted automatically not just on Twitter, but also on Facebook, LinkedIn, their company blog, their website, etc. Well, if you have followers on all those different sites, it means they could be hit with your same tweet in six or seven different channels. That's very annoying!

I've seen it happen—one of my advisors ended up hitting some of his users six different ways—including an email, a Facebook post, a LinkedIn update and so forth—with the same message on the same day. His *brother* called him up and said, "Seriously? You're sending all these messages over and over?" The brother just thought he was getting bombarded with emails—he didn't even know where they were all coming from.

That's why it's critical to understand the user's experience when it comes to receiving your content; irritation is probably not what you're going for. It's fine to post things across all platforms, as long as you make sure they're dynamic and not just the same message over and over.

UNDERSTANDING THE POWER OF LINKEDIN

The next step in accelerating your understanding of how to use social media for business purposes is to grasp the full power of LinkedIn.

LinkedIn is one of the fastest-growing and most influential social media platforms out there, with hundreds of millions of users. It added 16 million users in the first quarter of 2012 alone, and more and more business experts are advising people to get on board. Canaccord Genuity analyst Michael Graham said in a research note to clients, "We believe LinkedIn's member network is creating a pull that is solidifying its product set as a must-have for professionals."

B2B Companies that aren't engaged with LinkedIn can't maintain their large market share over the long term. Their competitors are out there on the site every day, privately talking to their customers and strengthening their connections to them. If you're not out there engaging proactively, getting inside the circle of trust with the markets you care about, somebody else will be.

The problem is that most business people view LinkedIn primarily as an employment site. It's not. It's actually an amazing business development platform, because it has hundreds of millions of people in its database, whose names you can search and sort to identify the professionals you want to be communicating with.

This makes it the dream tool for any direct marketer anywhere in the world. Whether you're looking for leads, new clients, sponsorship opportunities or new media engagements, or you just want to build an intimate and strong community, LinkedIn has the ideal setup. We use it to fill sales pipelines and events, hire new talent and, when it comes down to it, get new business—all through building an extremely targeted search list and LinkedIn community.

Again, most organizations only use LinkedIn for Human Resources objectives; they don't understand how it works as a business development tool. That's because they rely on LinkedIn to tell them what to do—but LinkedIn, unfortunately, doesn't currently offer what I would describe as a "high value proposition" to small businesses and professionals. Typically, LinkedIn will push its suite of tools, primarily advertising.

But here's the secret. The real power isn't in LinkedIn's advertising—it's in its inbox.

When you understand how to message on LinkedIn and use the feature to its fullest potential (within the LinkedIn rules, of course), you will have huge success. We've worked with organizations that have made as much as eight million dollars in only thirty days using the kind of highly-targeted campaigns I'm talking about here.

THE NEW RULES ARE THE NEW FUTURE

Communities are the future of marketing—and they are totally driven by social media. Every organization will become its own publishing entity—not in the sense that they will be putting out books right and left, but rather in that they'll be providing unique content that connects with each company's specific marketplace.

Here's another new rule. The traditional media (including TV, radio, and newspapers) and its one-way street approach to communication is going to render it less and less powerful. As that sphere loses influence, social media will gain it—only by the metric, however, by which *individuals* influence one another.

You see this everywhere on the Internet—every experience is continually being made to be a more specific one for each single user. Just check your Google search results when you're logged in to your Google account, log out, and check them again.

The difference? When you're logged in, Google accesses your past searches and social connections before providing you with a set of results relevant to your past searches. When you're logged out, you get the standardized results that everyone gets...when they're not logged into their own Google accounts.

Our social media circles will continue to influence what we see, what we find and what we search for. And you know what? *That's how it used to be.* These so-called "New Rules" are actually the same as the old ones. Human beings have always been tribal in behavior—this was just disrupted temporarily by our mass media culture. Now, the old rules are just coming to life online in a much more powerful way.

You can leverage that incredible power in your business today just by powering up your desktop computer, laptop, tablet or smartphone and building your own high-powered and targeted community.

If your organization is looking to establish more trust with your clients, build more credibility in the marketplace and take full advantage of the new rules of the social media game, please feel free to reach out to our organization at inquiry@linkedstrategies.com.

About Nathan

Nathan Kievman is a highly sought-after digital strategist, speaker and social media consultant and trainer. With a heavy focus on LinkedIn and B2B social media initiatives, he has generated more than $9 million in revenue for his clients directly from their social media programs. He uniquely combines business strategy, targeted objectives and ROI with social media, digital media and traditional marketing campaigns.

Considered one of the leading authorities on social media and LinkedIn, he has a robust following as the owner of the No. 1 LinkedIn Strategies Group on LinkedIn, and he's taught more than 35,000 people how to master the platform. He has authored three books on the topic, including the currently available "LinkedIn Mastery: An All-Inclusive Guide to Mastering LinkedIn," and he delivered the keynote adreess on social media strategy and led the advanced LinkedIn session at the National Speakers Association Winter Conference in 2011.

Companies hire Nathan for one of the following three reasons:

- to launch a digital or social media initiative

- to generate highly targeted leads through LinkedIn, and other social and digital channels

- to train employees on LinkedIn

He has consulted with Fortune 500 companies, Inc. 500 companies, well-known business leaders, and world-renowned speakers and authors, as well as many small to mid-sized businesses.

Nathan holds two master's degrees, in business and in sports administration, from the highly acclaimed sports program at Ohio University. He and his beautiful wife Leah have three vibrant children and currently reside in the Cleveland/Akron area of Ohio.

CHAPTER 7

Millions On Automation

By Mikkel Pitzner

Until fairly recently, I ran the largest limousine service company in Denmark. When I say I ran it, I mean that I owned it and had other people running it for me. Instead of being tied up all the time with the day-to-day business operations, such as order processing and sending out confirmations, invoicing, directing staff, and dealing with vendors, I had a team of employees who took care of all these matters for me, from directing all the chauffeurs to handling the all-important logistical task of allocating cars and chauffeurs for jobs (which also involved managing the constant changes in the schedule resulting from airplane delays, customers changing their itineraries, and so on). This setup meant that I could be away from the business, not only physically but mentally, exploring other opportunities and diving into other projects and businesses. Indeed, whenever I worked on the limousine business, I was doing exactly that: working *on* the business rather than *in* it.

This situation was not created intentionally, but rather came about because I bought the company at a time when I was employed as the CEO of another company, and I had to dedicate my time and service to my original company. So from the very beginning, I had to have a team of other people who could handle the limousine service business, since otherwise it could not continue to service its customers or even exist.

Then on evenings and weekends, I could work on the direction in which I wanted to take the limousine company and tweak certain parameters, looking at prices, terms and conditions, preparing sales efforts and direct mailings, and more. This arrangement worked quite well. For some years, with the right team, it worked really, really well; at other times, I faced some challenges, both from trouble getting the team aligned with my wishes and directions, and external pressures due to the market, demand fluctuations and competition from other operators.

The fantastic thing was that this setup gave me choices and freedom, and all the while the company was generating income for me. At times I would actually be virtually absent from the business and thinking so little about it that it was almost a joke. One of the Chief Operational Managers I employed there for a number of years used to say to me that I "was just sitting with my feet in the pool sipping drinks with small umbrellas." When she first said this, I was a little offended, but I soon came to realize that it she was somewhat correct (truth hurts sometimes). Though I did work, I had more freedom than most business owners to choose how to spend my time and in which areas to focus.

To recap, I was involved with the limousine service business for 16 years, 14 of which I owned it privately, before I sold the business towards the end of 2010. Yet, when I try tally up just how much time I spent in that business' physical offices, I believe that it's no more than 60 days. 60 days in a total of 16 years! This is not something that makes me particularly proud—it would have been better to have more interactions with my employees and display more interest in them— but it does illustrate what you can achieve with the right setup.

What I came to learn from my years with this setup is that you can, to some extent, set up your business or businesses on what I call automation. This arrangement enabled me to hold another high-end job in a top position, while running my own business and even allowing me to engage in further new businesses on top of that, so that in the end I actually had a small portfolio of different (and as it happened, unrelated) businesses and projects going on at the same time. I did work more than 60 days on my limousine business during those 16 years, but I certainly wasn't engaged in full-time work with it the entire time. Now, I do believe I could possibly have gotten better results with the business had I been more personally and directly involved in it (remember, nobody cares more about your money than you do), but I wouldn't have had the opportunity to get involved in many other businesses during the same period, and thus would not have the businesses or involvement in businesses that I have today. Some of these other businesses have proven to have much more potential and delivered much bigger results than those that seemed possible in my limousine business.

That's why, when we sold off the other company I'd been running and I ended my role as its CEO, I was able to decide where to focus next, and chose not to go into the limousine business full-time. I could have opted to work more personally in that company, and zero in on its strategy and potential, and this might have seemed to be the most natural next step. It would have probably offered me some fun and excitement, as well as the chance to interact with employees and customers to a much greater extent than I had in my "remote control" position. But I realized that I actually really enjoyed being able to engage myself in so many other businesses, and I chose not to go this route. I also feared that if I had stepped into the limousine business on an operational level, I would have ended up quickly being a kind of slave to it, becoming a too-important part of the daily function of the business, and all of a sudden I would have to relegate all my other opportunities and projects to the evenings and weekends. In fact, I'm pretty certain that this would have come to pass. As I said, I'm sure being more personally involved in the limousine business would have been fun and satisfying on many levels, but I wanted so much more. So I continued with the arrangement I'd been using for the previous four years.

As I've progressed in my life and career, and continued to realize the potential of automating a business or businesses, I have been even more enthusiastic about the idea. Thus, I have deliberately engaged myself in a serious study of how and what is possible with automation. What my research has revealed astounds me again and again. The possibilities are almost limitless, and they apply to many different types of businesses, products, and services.

As I said, I have thoroughly studied the topic of automation for the past three to four years. I've looked at some of the most successful entrepreneurs, and deconstructed what they did, how they did it and how someone else could apply their model to his or her own business. I was able to draw a number of particularly interesting conclusions from my study, including:

1. First of all, almost anybody can do it. Many of the highly successful people who have run a large part of their business by automation are just really ordinary folks. Many of them have had barely any education. Some of them are not special in any particular way, and they don't possess any specific skills that you couldn't develop yourself.

2. For many of them, setting up their business was not exactly free, but it certainly didn't require much money. In fact,

3. Many of them had no money at all when they began.

4. Some of them found new ways to utilize tools and systems to leverage themselves and amplify their scope and results to a greater extent than would have been possible just a few years before.

5. Many of them have very few employees, or none at all.

6. Their products and services can vary widely and may be completely unrelated.

7. Sometimes, their results are astoundingly big.

8. You can utilize most of the tools and ideas in brick-and-mortar or service businesses, as well as in strictly online ones.

There are many, many more amazing and surprising advantages. And what is most mind-blowing, I have recently learned, is that you might be able to set up your business on evergreen automation. This means that once you have done all the hard work of setting it up, then it can run almost by itself continuously, making you constant income without too much intervention and administration.

If you are not excited about this opportunity and what it means for you, then you should be! You can emulate the steps taken by these successful individuals and build similar opportunities, regardless of your background or *"your story"* or perhaps even because of them. You can model a successful path for your future using some of the same paths and techniques, regardless of your product or service, and with particular limitations in sight at the moment.

I had my remote-controlled and automated business experience with a brick-and–mortar, physical kind of business, but I've found that online businesses can offer even greater opportunities, if for no other reason than that you can quickly cater to an exponentially bigger market across borders. In particular, if you focus on selling information and expertise, you might see some impressive results, big sales and very satisfied customers, all with relatively low costs and few employees to worry about.

Now I'm not saying that all of this is easy; it does require a serious effort and hard work along the way. What I am saying is that you can now create a great business, utilizing new tools that can propel your results, automate your deliveries, and communicate with your market in ways that were not possible just five years ago. And this technology is rapidly advancing even further. Many of these tools are relatively inexpensive and becoming easier and easier to use, even if you aren't a technical expert. And new information that will help you to progress down this path is becoming available every day. Some of it is free, but more of it is for a price, often one that is much lower than the value of the content you get. Trainers and experts are sharing their knowledge and experience, and communities are helping one another to move forward instead of seeing one another as nasty competitors.

What makes this even better is that your customers are really happy to find great information that will help them achieve their goals. In fact, if you do right by your customers, you can actually go beyond satisfying them to building your own "tribe" who is willing and even happy to support your future endeavors and products.

I refer several times in this chapter to the online information business opportunity available to most people who have a special skill or knowledge from which others can benefit. By now, you may be thinking: "What do I know that I could build this kind of a business with?" You may even be shaking your head, saying to yourself: "What this guy is telling me is all fine and dandy, but I don't know anything about anything that people would pay me for." But trust me: there is a market out there for almost anything. To give you an example, there is at least one individual I know who has built an online information business in the area of quilting. Yes, the art of sewing together pieces of fabric into blankets. I'm sure there many even more curious but just as successful information businesses out there.

The book you are currently reading is the result of collaboration with one of my mentors, Robert G. Allen. Indeed, it's quite possible that you picked up this book because you have heard of him, or even read one of his great books before. But if you're not familiar with him, then I can tell you that he became very famous for his brilliant real estate investing strategies, specifically buying properties with no money down.

A little further down the line, Allen began to formularize his methods, and packaged and sold them as information products online. He met with huge success, building to an automated business and income streams. Eventually he licensed this information and training out to a company, and now receives recurring and growing revenues without having to do any more work. Later on, he built up his product information business in other areas utilizing tools available to all of us, and he's achieved results that dwarf his previous results. If I'm not mistaken, Allen has made more money from this automated business than from his real estate investments.

Will everybody make millions using these strategies and trying to emulate their results? Probably not, but even if you could just make a few extra thousand dollars a month through automation, couldn't you use that money? What about automating certain communications and marketing channels of your brick-and-mortar business in ways that will not only take off a burden off your shoulders, but also leave your customers with an improved experience?

The opportunities are endless. You just need to go and see how you can utilize the tools to make your business really soar, and provide you with the lifestyle you always imagined. These are exciting times. This is your time too, if you choose to take action.

If you are as excited as I am, and you're interested in learning more about the tools and how you can take advantage of these possibilities, and to get a free gift, visit www.theautomatedmillionaire.com/freegift.

About Mikkel

Mikkel Pitzner was born on March 3, 1968. He received a Bachelor of Science in Economics from University College of London (England) with honors in 1991. He has completed shorter intense courses in Political Science and Game Theory at Columbia University in New York, and a business course for CEOs at Harvard Business School in Massachusetts.

He is a serial and parallel entrepreneur, investor, and professional board member in Denmark, Sweden and the US (who currently sits on nine boards spanning diverse industries), as well as a marketing and social media expert and consultant, mastermind, and dreamer extraordinaire.

He is a partner in the unique marketing and trailer rental company Freetrailer, which currently operates throughout Denmark and Sweden with more countries to come. He is a partner at Aksel & Ko, a company that can find that special gimmick or solution corporations need for their marketing strategies.

Pitzner is originally from Denmark, where he used to run what became the fourth-largest car rental company and a leasing company whose size he doubled and locations he quadrupled. Until recently, he owned and operated the largest limousine service company in Denmark, whose profits he managed to grow 3200% during the first year of ownership alone. The company served the most discerning clientele, including no fewer than three U.S. presidents—George W. Bush, Bill Clinton and Barack Obama, the last one during the United Nations Climate Change Conference in 2009 during which the company serviced more than 200 limousines to the U.S. Embassy in Copenhagen, along with numerous other embassies, countries, royalties, celebrities, multi-conglomerates, and so on. Pitzner also successfully ran an import and distribution company of scuba diving equipment until that company was sold to a German distributor.

Mikkel Pitzner is also a best-selling author and speaker who teaches entrepreneurs how to create a business that will provide them with the lifestyle they choose while taking them off the treadmill of their jobs. Pitzner has been featured on CNBC, ABC, NBC, CNNMONEY.com, Fox News, CBS News, and in the *Wall Street Journal, Fortune, Fast Company, SmartMoney* and *USA Today.* He was also recently a guest on the "Brian Tracy Show."

Mikkel Pitzner currently resides in Florida with his beautiful wife Olga and twenty-one-month-old son Gabriel, and they're expecting a baby girl. He's building four new business ventures simultaneously, while helping a local manufacturer in a struggling and challenging economy.

CHAPTER 7

The New Rules of Building a Team

By Michael Hellickson

You need a professional Disney cartoonist to draw you something? Done.

You want one of the world's greatest violinists to teach your kid how to play using Skype? No problem.

Maybe you'd just like someone to call you up in the morning and tell you how great you are. Sure thing.

Oh, and if you happen to want expert accounting services, bookkeeping, telemarketing, web design, data entry or any type of business or office skills whatsoever—at pennies on the dollar, 100% satisfaction guaranteed, without the stress or extra payroll expenses?

Consider it done.

In the world of Virtual Assistants (or VAs), the world is your employment pool, and virtually any high or low-level skill you're looking for is available, at an amazing price and at your convenience.

I revolutionized my business by using VAs. And you can revolutionize yours by using VAs, too.

BOOSTING MY BOTTOM LINE—
BY $85,000 A MONTH

I don't know if I was born to sell real estate, but I certainly didn't major in it. That's because I was already a successful real estate agent before I finished high school. I was a top agent while I was still taking algebra. I became so successful that I was actually named the #13 real estate agent in the U.S. by the Wall Street Journal (I was actually #1 for a period of time)!

Of course, in 2007, what happened to the entire housing industry happened to me. The bottom fell out of the market, I lost over $100,000 in commissions in one month and all I had was a handful of unsellable listings.

I decided I had to go big or go home. While I had been consistently successful in my field, I knew it was time to take things to the next level so that 2007 couldn't happen to me again. However, I also knew that I needed the right team to help me reach that next level. I had to make a big investment and take a big risk. I talked it over with my wife, and we took a big leap of faith.

Fortunately, we landed safely on the other side. With my new team in place, I actually achieved even more success in this new economy, handling over 417 short sales and retail listings, and more than 325 REO sales and listings, all within a ten-month period.

Now, however, I had a whole new problem. Even though I was generating more income than ever before, I never knew if I was going to be making hundreds of thousands of dollars each month—or losing the same amount.

The reason was glaringly obvious—because I had hired so many people, I was looking at a **monthly** payroll of over $123,517! I had beefed up my support staff to 44 employees, which allowed me to sell more properties. If I were to reduce that staff, I would lose a lot of valuable revenue—I was faced with a Catch-22.

As I was pondering what to do, several friends told me that they successfully worked with Virtual Assistants. It seemed strange to hire people an ocean away to do local work—but the cost savings appeared to be dramatic, and my friends were telling me I could access a higher quality talent pool by hiring globally. So, reluctantly I hired my first VA, figuring the person could assist one of my current managers so that it would be no big deal if it didn't work out.

But it did work out. Spectacularly. My manager **loved** working with the VA.

And so I hired two more. One did an amazing job, and the other not-so-amazing. So we replaced that person. The new one, again, did the trick. All of a sudden, I saw the light, and understood the new rules of the game when it came to hiring staff.

VAs eliminated the drama that can often accompany a large staff. They made things more efficient. They worked harder than the regular staff, and, most importantly, they made it possible to cut that $125,000 payroll down to $40,000 a month. I could cut 68% of personnel costs each month (an $85,000 savings). That meant I no longer had to worry about having a month end in the red.

VAs changed my business—and they changed my life.

They can do the same for you.

THE VA ADVANTAGE

I want to further explain more of the important benefits you might be able to see when you use VAs—it's not just a matter of payroll savings. Employing VAs can bring so many other collateral advantages to you and your business.

But let's start with those payroll expenses. With VAs, suddenly you're getting just as much, if not more, work done, **and** you're *not* paying:

- Salaries or wages
- Employment taxes

- Workers' Comp

- Vacation days

- Sick days

- Health insurance premiums

You're also not paying your employees to chat around the water cooler or get into petty feuds that disrupt your operation. People are complicated, and when you put a bunch of them together from nine to five, you can end up with more drama than Shakespeare could have ever imagined. In contrast, VAs just do the work—and you don't have to deal with anything beyond actual job performance. Sometimes, it pays to be an ocean away.

Also, remember that you not only have to compensate your local employees—you also have to provide them with a physical workplace and take care of all the accompanying expenses. With VAs, that's not a concern, which means you're no longer paying for:

- Office space

- Office supplies

- Office insurance

- Telephone/Internet costs

- Office equipment (computers, copiers, etc.)

- Energy costs (air conditioning, heating, etc.)

I did away with that entire infrastructure. With an entirely virtual operation, I no longer needed it—and I was still able to sell hundreds and hundreds of properties a year.

Now, let's look beyond how VAs might save you money, at how they might even make you money.

Many of you have paid for a multitude of marketing seminars and books, and you often think about using the techniques and tricks you've learned from these valuable resources. At the same time, you don't have the manpower to put a lot of these important marketing plans in action, nor do you have the time to make those plans happen by yourself.

That's where VAs can really make a difference. They can provide an incredible variety of marketing skills—especially in the online arena—at an incredibly low cost. For example, you can find VAs who excel at:

- Telemarketing
- Web design and development
- Logo design
- Research projects
- Video editing
- Article and blog writing and posting
- Google AdWords
- Social Media (Facebook, Twitter, LinkedIn, etc.)
- Copywriting
- Brochures and Flyers
- SEO
- Transcription services

Tedious marketing chores that might drive you crazy or be too expensive to hire out can easily be handled by a qualified VA—one who makes sure that no balls are dropped. Your business gets consistently promoted according to the plan you create, and your marketing profile gets a recurring boost.

You have to love that.

IT'S STILL *YOUR* BUSINESS!

If you haven't considered using VAs before, you may feel a little strange about having work that used to be done a few feet from your desk, if not at it, done remotely. You may feel like you're giving away control of your company, which was one of my big fears.

What I discovered, though, is that I am still very much in charge. The work is still being regularly reviewed, either by me or someone who works for me. I even have time tracking software that tracks EVERY MINUTE my VA's are working! I can see screen shots of everything they do, AND get automatic reports on a daily and weekly basis that alert me to any potential time wasted! I bet you're not getting that from your local staff. When necessary, I can even replace a VA with another one.

Since by definition, VAs are always somewhere else, it doesn't matter where you are—you're able to put them to work for you. This is especially beneficial if you are contemplating frequent travel, or even a move (to a warmer climate, perhaps!) in the future. You can hire VAs to do anything that needs to be done—as long as they don't have to be physically present to do it.

I can't hire a VA to show a house for me. However, I can and do hire VAs to complete all sorts of real estate paperwork, as well as handle accounting, marketing and other day-to-day duties. The difference is it gets done without my having to worry about it. (Remember, even if I am not watching them, my software is!)

Another great way to use a VA is as a gatekeeper—they can check your emails, take your calls, look after your schedule, and send you reminders and do all the other things that a regular assistant does. I have a VA whose entire job is to call warm leads and prospective clients and set up appointments for me to talk to them. This way, my daily schedule is full of people who are anxious and expecting to talk to me about what I do.

And in case you're concerned, yes, VAs do speak English, in fact, most of mine speak PERFECT, ACCENT FREE English! You even can hire a VA for full-time or part-time work, or for even as little as 2.5 hours a week.

WORK *ON* YOUR BUSINESS, NOT *IN* YOUR BUSINESS

You've probably heard the expression "Work ON your business, not IN your business!" Using VAs is the perfect way to do just that. With VAs quickly and efficiently handling the dreary tasks that weigh us all down, we're free to look at ways to expand our existing business as well as explore new opportunities.

As a matter of fact, VAs became a new opportunity for me: using them got me so excited about their potential for everybody else that I left my ridiculously profitable real estate business and founded Virtual Assistant Staffing™, the world's leading headhunting agency. We find, hire and train the top international VAs to provide the same kinds of savings and business advantages that I'd benefited from.

We provide this kind of valuable help to companies in corporate America, mom-and-pop businesses like real estate agencies, investors, national speakers (including some of the authors of this book), and businesses of all other shapes and sizes. As I write this, we're working on a contract to place some top secret clearance level help for two government agencies with three letter names, believe it or not.

The vast majority of businesses need and will benefit from the kind of talented teams you can assemble with VAs; they just think they can't afford the expense or can't find people with the right skills. They're wrong on both counts. You can and will build a team to lead your company to the next level, just like I did with my real estate operation.

What's been really eye-opening, though, is seeing how much value VAs add to a wide variety of other industries as well. My experience running this company has shown me the awesome range of talents that VAs provide in different business sectors. When I said at the beginning of this chapter that I can give you access to a Disney quality cartoonist or a world-class musician, I wasn't kidding. There is an astonishing amount of high-level talent available at very low rates worldwide. You just have to know where to look and how to look and choose the best candidate, and fortunately, I do.

I trust VAs so much that, when we have a booth at a trade show, I man it virtually. I mean this literally: we have a tablet PC at the counter and a VA who interacts with visitors via Skype, just to demonstrate how well the process works. I don't even have to worry about the tablet PC being stolen, as Samsung and Microsoft were smart enough to include a LoJack-style feature that allows it to be tracked via GPS if it goes missing. In that event, it can also be remotely disabled to protect my data. By not having to pay to get staff to and from events, I have saved literally tens of thousands of dollars in airfare and hotel costs.

WORKING SUCCESSFULLY WITH VAS

I don't mean to infer that working with VAs is a magical process. There are still a few important steps to creating successful and productive relationships with them that I have learned over the past few years.

Despite the "Virtual" part of their title, VAs are very much flesh-and-blood human beings. Just like other employees, they have different skill levels and pay rates. You will also need to train them in the specific demands of your business, and hold them accountable for doing the work the way as you specify and on your timetable. To make this happen, you need to communicate clearly and consistently, just as you would with any other employee.

The neat thing is that over time they do become just like other employees, only better! That means, as you get to know them, you can reassign them, promote them or, if necessary, replace them. They are truly members of your team, and you can manage them to victory.

Our company helps our clients with that effort by providing you with what a Relationship Manager who makes sure your VA experience starts off on the best possible foot. We even let you try out your VA for 40 hours FOR FREE to ensure he or she is the right long-term person for your team. (This offer may be discontinued without notice.) If the first person we place with your team isn't absolutely fantastic, we will replace him or her, for free. I can't guarantee that the first VA we find for you will make a perfect long-term match for your team, but I can absolutely guarantee that you won't pay us a dime until you and I agree that we've found the right person.

Running a profitable company is difficult in this day and age. Between the weak economy, taxes and other challenges, today's business leaders need all the help they can get. VAs provide that help at an unbeatable price. Consider trying out a VA with your business; take back your profitability, your time, your freedom, and your life. Just like I've found the key to virtual success, and so many other owners of profitable businesses have joined me, I know you will too.

About Michael

Michael Hellickson is currently the CEO of Virtual Assistant Staffing™, one of the fastest-growing virtual staffing agencies in the world. With over 1000 people in the process of getting their first VA, Virtual Assistant Staffing is the way to go if you want to find a VA with the confidence and assurance that you get the right person, and to avoid the headache of the hiring and firing process.

Virtual Assistant Staffing is the Rolls-Royce of the virtual assisting industry. As the world's leading virtual assistant recruiting firm, the company specializes in helping business find, hire and train top talent from around the globe at an average savings of more than 67% over hiring local employees!

Companies hire Virtual Assistant Staffing for one of the following reasons:

1. To find world-class talent at affordable prices

2. To test-drive new hires with absolutely no risk (we give 40 free hours)

3. To save money on staff and employees

4. To outsource the entire interviewing and recruiting process for free

5. To find talent that may not exist in their local markets

Michael Hellickson recently transitioned from the real estate industry, in which he'd built a multi-million dollar business as a real estate agent, eventually becoming the nation's #1 real estate agent. During his career, Hellickson has spoken to and coached thousands of students and organizations nationwide.

Michael has been featured on several national television and radio programs and networks, including:

- CNBC
- Fox Business Network
- "Glenn Beck"
- "The Dave Ramsey Show"

• And many other local & regional programs

Michael, his wife Tara, and their two amazing children make their home in Bonney Lake, Washington, where they are active in their church, sports, outdoor activities and various philanthropic efforts. To "test drive" one of Michael's VA's for FREE, visit www.VirtualAssistantStaffing.com/NewRules

CHAPTER 9

Rules?!? WTF*??

***NOT what you think it means, it's Wealth,
The Formula. However, I use it for a LOT of things.**

By Marco Kozlowski

New Rules? HA! By nature, I am a rule breaker, which has been my greatest asset, and perhaps one of my biggest flaws. As a serial entrepreneur, I don't believe in rules. And weren't "Rules" meant to be broken, anyway?

I didn't build, buy or sell a dozen or so businesses over the last two years, starting from less than scratch, without breaking a few rules along the way...

Everyone in this book has their own spin on success; however, I'd like to make you a promise and offer an incentive for you to follow some of the rules I have laid out for you in this chapter.

Would you like to generate more income in the next 17 months than you did in the past 17 months AND at the same time give more back to the causes you believe in? Giving back is a rule that I never break, and funnily enough, in the two years since I've adopted this philosophy, I have had more abundance in all areas of my life, for which I am grateful. **(Rule No. 2)**

If you want outstanding results like my own, please consider that without applying what I have set out, nothing will happen.

The definition of insanity is doing the same thing over and over again and expecting different results. Are you repeating the same patterns, never changing what you do or who you do it with, and yet wondering why your life isn't growing?

I really want to help you. **(Rule No. 1)**

I find it really challenging to contribute only one concept to this book—just ONE rule. Only ONE whose application can take you from pauper to prince, mini to mighty and zero to hero. It's a cycle that I have gone through many times in my own life—from when I was a struggling musician looking for coins in friends' couches to feed my four young kids (WTF?) to real estate mogul, within a few short years of laser-focused action, to having it all disappear overnight when a series of unfortunate events including a perfect storm of bitter divorce and the real estate crash arrived all at once.

So, I'll break the rules I was given, and give you the important ones from my rule book, which I suspect will help you get wealthy, stay wealthy, and lose the whole "lost it all" phase that so many of us mavericks tend to cycle through....unless, of course, you need the lesson, in which case I can't help you there.

Ask me how I know this.

I've made more and lost more than many see in a lifetime, and I've been humble enough to learn the very hard, yet very valuable, lessons that life and the universe throw at you just to see if you are paying attention.

At some point, we all feel like the ant under that snotty-nosed kid's magnifying glass on a perfect summer day. . . just when we think everything is going great...ZAP! Shit happens to all of us. It's going to continue to happen, and you have two choices: You can learn, grow and win from the experience given to you, or lie down in a fetal position, suck your thumb and give up.

This choice is 100% up to you. You have to take responsibility. **(Rule No. 7)**

"Be nice to your enemies—you created them."

So that's Rule No. 1: Learn from YOUR mistakes. Own them—they are yours.

You are exactly where you designed yourself to be.

You got the grades that got you the education that got you the job that allowed you to get the car and the stuff and the wife and all the other "stuff" you have now.

You created that. So if there isn't enough in your bank account, your business is struggling and you work so hard that you don't understand how your child already has facial hair (hopefully, not the girl), it's all because of you, my friend. . .

All of YOUR choices up until THIS point got you here.

However, your past does NOT equal your future. **(Rule No. 22)**

You can change the course of your life the INSTANT you make the decision to do so.

HA! This sounds like something that's easier said then done—I never said the rules were EASY. So instead of focusing on the hard ones (like changing your spouse) in the short time I have here, let's focus on something I've been studying, living and breathing through constant action for the last few years that has really impacted my life financially, with more time and abundance (wealth).

With your permission (of course), I would like to share with you the simplified formula for wealth that I have distilled for your immediate consumption. Sound good?

Let's talk about your favorite topic for a second: yes, you.

Are you looking at your bank account right now and gasping because you have way too much money?

Why not?

Ever wonder why some people who started out in the poorest countries and started from scratch or less than nothing have been able to survive and become some of the wealthiest people on earth?

If they did it, why can't you? WTF??

You went to the right school, got the right education, got the right job—or started the right business—but you have no freedom. You can't take every other month off, or things fall apart, don't they?

So what went wrong?

Don't believe the lies. **(Rule No. 3)**

Are the rich getting richer?

Are the wealthy working hard, or working smart?

Are wealthy people working 9-5 jobs?

Did the wealthy go to school to get a job to become sheep-like people?

Not a chance…

The wealthy lie to us and have us all brainwashed to work hard in order to build a society that feeds and serves THEM. (They are getting wealthier, my friend.)

You even were told that "time is money"!

That's preposterous—time is NOTHING like money. That's a saying elites use to get you to work for them for YEARS at a "fair" wage so that the owners of the organization can enjoy their freedom.

The workers work while the rich get wealthier.

I have never heard any story of a man drawing his last breath and wishing he had worked harder, or made more money. But I believe that we all wish for more time.

So how, pray tell, is time ANYTHING like money?

It's not. They are apples and oranges.

"Great Marco," you're probably thinking. "Now what?"

What do you think separates the wealthy from the broke? The haves from the have nots? Where you want to be from where you are?

Education? I know a lot of extremely educated people who are totally broke.

Action? You can take action, but still be broke.

Money? You don't need money to make money—I wrote a book on that topic, too.

What is it?

Who told you, "Go to school," "Get a job," and "Work hard," anyway? Your parents? Are they wealthy? It's not their fault if they're not— they were lied to as well. This been going on for years, but you can break the cycle whenever you chose to. Many have done so, and I believe in you.

Change your behavior. **(Rule No. 16)**

If you start behaving like a successful person does, then you will automatically have the same results.

Let's look at some of the cool little behaviors of extremely successful people, so that we can apply them to ourselves.

Do you like sports?

Who in a football team makes more money: the players or the owner?

Obviously, the owner—but what is his function?

If he took a few months off, what would happen to the organization? Nothing, really.

But if a star player decided to take a week, month or year off with- out telling anyone, what would happen? They would be suspended, or fired without pay.

So the owners make more money, don't face the risk of injury, don't have to show up if they don't want to, don't get replaced as they get older, and get to have an abundant life to enjoy as their players are working hard to make them wealthy!

Is this how you designed your life to be?

Are you the owner of your team? Or the player? Are you your own boss, and is your boss a jerk? Are you making yourself do everything, playing all the positions on your team and yet wondering why you have no time, no money and no life?

If your life stinks, it's simply because your behavior stinks.

Success is a team sport. **(Rule No. 8)**

You must have the right players in the key positions in your life and business to complement your success, rather than pull it back. If you have the wrong players on your team, the team loses. It's that simple.

Imagine having an infrastructure of people to find and attract new business for you, ones who don't get paid until they've done what they've promised to do. I'm talking about a 100% performance-based team, all of whose members NEED to win the game WITH you.

I'm talking about the phone ringing off the hook with new costumers, the best sales people converting those new leads into raving fans, and having more business than you know what to do with—and all you had to do was put the team together.

It's not a dream: It's one of my superpowers. **(Rule No. 47: find your superpower)**

In fact, I have a free gift for you: an ebook to help you find the right players. I'd love to help you build a team WITHOUT PAYING THEM UPFRONT, allowing you to turn your passion into profits with the best people out there for you.

Go to WTFRules.com to get your complimentary ebook that will teach you how to build a team of people who want to make you wealthy.

Speaking of wealth—

Do you really want financial freedom??

What is financial abundance? It really varies from person to person. For you, it might be $10,000 a month, for others $100,000 a day. We all choose our level of poverty.

So for me to tell you what "making it" is would be out of line—you are in a unique situation and must be treated as such.

However, would making an extra million in the next 17 months be OK with you? A million that you didn't have to sacrifice 17 months of life with your family for, but rather 17 months of steadily changing your behavior, building a team, finding your superpower and turning on a machine that makes you wealthy whether you like it or not—rain or shine, sunrise to sunset.

Did I get your attention yet?

Before you call BS on my statement, let's first figure out what a million really looks like, and how it's even possible for me to make such a seemingly ridiculous statement without really knowing you.

RULE NO. 1: HELP PEOPLE FIRST

In this economy, do people need help?

They do. If you have a group of people who need help, you help them. If you solve their problems and impact their lives so that they need to continue their relationships with you, what will the result be?

You got it: abundance.

Money is only a result of how many people we have helped and at what level. If I were to help 1000 people at a $1000 price point, that is a million bucks, my friends. Yes, it's that easy.

The most important rule—the one that is unbreakable, non-negotiable and crucial if you want to make a HUGE impact on others including yourself and your family—is to help people.

The more people you help, the more you affect their lives, the better solutions you provide for others, the more money you make. It's a byproduct of that behavior that you can't escape.

You just have to figure out how to help more people, i.e., what solutions can you provide. (I've created a few exercises that can help you figure these out—I would really love to help YOU, too.)

But be cautious in picking something that you think is amazing. No matter how awesome WE think they are, any of the ideas we have will fall flat unless OTHERS see the need for them. It's not what WE think is amazing that's important. (This is **Rule No. 35**, and it *can* be broken occasionally.)

Let's recap:

If you were to change your behavior TODAY, get my free ebook to help you find your superpower, which would enable you to build support structures of key people to help you help others—and then impact 1000 people in the next 17 months:

- You would help a lot of people
- You would have others doing the stuff you're bad at
- You would have more time with your family
- You would feel more fulfilled
- You would enjoy the finer things in life

The finer things, of course, are time AND money. And THAT is wealth.

About Marco

Marco Kozlowski is considered to be one of the world's leading experts on delegation and systems process engineering. He is currently an owner in a wide variety of successful companies. From his work with holistic centers and cancer research facilities to private business consulting to recording companies, Marco's methodology has delivered proven results. His business success began in the niche market of luxury real estate, where he built a multi-million-dollar company from scratch and without start-up capital. Marco then leveraged the knowledge he obtained to systematize and solidify the business process system that he teaches to business owners across the globe today.

WTF!: A title as bold as Marco.

Wealth: The Formula teaches business owners how to structure their businesses in a way that maximizes profit and compensation for the business owner and every single member of the team. WTF is Marco's codified and proven system for building wealth in any business or industry. This is the same formula that he developed himself and used to build 12 multi-million-dollar companies, companies with only a few employees or none whatsoever.

That's right! In the vein of Sir Richard Branson, Marco has mastered the art of delegation. His delegation methodology allows him to spend more time doing what he loves to do: HELPING OTHERS! His businesses run effectively and efficiently, while he is able to live a life that he is passionate about.

Marco, who entered adulthood as a struggling musician, and the father of four children, is now known to audiences and media outlets alike as "The Top Powerful Speaker in the World." Marco uses his speaking talents to educate other business owners on the absolute best methodology for optimizing the profits of all involved parties. The formula for wealth has been identified and tested. His revolutionary system allows other business owners to create the same stability and success he has experienced.

CHAPTER 10

The New Investment Rules: Breaking Out of the Traditional Investor Box

By Corbin Cowan

If you invested $1 in the Standard & Poor's 500 on December 31, 1999, you ended up with exactly 90 cents on December 31, 2009.

According to *USA Today*, the beginning ten years of this new millennium was the first calendar decade ever that ended up giving investors a negative return from the S&P 500 stock index (and yes, this does include the Great Depression during the 1930s). This was despite a 23.5% gain in the year 2009—imagine if that rebound hadn't happened! Or even worse if you sold at the bottom and did not experience the rebound after the government bailout had been approved.

The Wall Street meltdown toward the end of 2008 changed many people's perceptions about the safety of their stock market investments, including mine. It sent me on a single-minded mission to find a solution that would finally bring peace of mind to the average investor. What I discovered completely surprised me, and has caused me to completely change the way that I work with clients. I no longer consider myself a financial adviser, but rather an investor coach.

In my opinion, the financial services industry is one of the biggest conspiracies that exists in today's world. The worst part about this industry is that they really don't try to hide this fact. The first thing I do when I meet with a new client as an investor coach is to write 99.9 on the whiteboard in my office. When they ask what it means, I answer, "99.9% of all advisers and brokers are nothing more than sophisticated gamblers."

There is overwhelming evidence and research that stock picking and market timing are two of the biggest causes of investor losses, and yet this is exactly what media outlets, including magazines and news publications, push. What I discovered is that stock selection accounts for less than 5% of the return on a portfolio. Don't take my word for it, though, look at the research done by Harry Markowitz on Modern Portfolio Theory, which gained a little bit of respect in 1990 when he won a little award called the Nobel Memorial Prize in Economic Sciences. This may seem like an incredible statement to make in today's volatile market, but I believe that with the right education you can achieve total peace of mind about your portfolio. Before I explain why this is true, I'd like to reveal exactly why I've become a believer in this long-term investment strategy, and why this portfolio design is so attractive.

THE SYSTEM: HITTING A DEAD END

I started my first investment company while I was still an undergraduate at the University of Colorado, all because of a dare. I had a professor who had just joined the faculty from the Wharton School at the University of Pennsylvania. Students at Wharton had started their own investment firm, and this professor wanted to know who was brave enough to do it at my school.

I was the guy who raised his hand.

This was in the late 1990s, when you could do no wrong in the market. We raised money by selling shares in the new company to fellow students, and we managed the portfolio ourselves. The business structure was solid; so solid, in fact, that the investment company still operates at the school, giving current students their own opportunity to learn about investing in stocks.

Of course, if I went back there now, I'd tell them not to bother: you can't pick winners and losers with any certainty. After graduation, I became gradually disillusioned with the investment establishment. At first, however, I determined that I wanted to continue working in the conventional financial services world. I educated myself about investing and strategy, and began to make a study of how the wealthy invest to create even more wealth.

That's when I began to see for myself that the whole financial services industry is a big conspiracy—and a rip-off. These big institutions have created a huge system that exists mainly to rob the American public, one that is built around various marketing efforts and investment products that allow these institutions to collect recurring fees on the huge amount of money Americans put into the market. If you calculated the amount of money that is being ripped off from the Main Street investor, Wall Street would make Bernie Madoff look like Robin Hood.

And that's when I also observed that really wealthy people don't get rich by investing in stocks. People like Warren Buffett made their fortunes by buying companies, not mutual fund shares, and then putting right management teams in place to re-energize those companies and raise their stock prices. That made me re-evaluate everything I had taught myself about conventional investing, and start to look at different and more satisfying ways I could serve my clients.

But there was one last painful lesson I had to learn. In 2005, I had the chance to get into the oil industry when it was red-hot, and crude oil climbed quickly to a record high of $147 a barrel. When it dropped back to $35 in the space of ninety days, I lost everything, and had to refocus on what was important.

And that's when I decided to become an investor coach. I'm as fully licensed as any other financial adviser, but instead of relying on the same old investment strategies, I've connected with individuals who have the same kind of vision as I do. We've found tremendous opportunities working with high-net-worth individuals, and positioned ourselves so that our clients can take advantage of the economy rather than being taken advantage of by it.

THE NEW WAY TO INVEST

As I mentioned, I have a fundamental problem with how financial services are sold in this country, because I believe they're sold for the benefit of the financial institutions creating the products and not necessarily for the benefit of Main Street investors, who compose the bulk of investors in the U.S.

This model worked fine when the market kept going up and up. But now, it doesn't function so well. However, all a traditional investment adviser knows is the stock market. If it's not publicly traded and purchased through their clearing desk, they don't know anything about it, including how to take advantage of it. The trouble is, this incredible lack of diversification is what has led to ten years of going nowhere in the market. The good news is that there's a whole new world of opportunity that's been created, and it's a world you want to be a part of if you want to experience any real peace of mind.

My partners and I have created a systematic and predictable approach to investing that we believe best positions our clients to be successful. We make it a point to fully educate our clients about our market-based investment strategies, as well as alternative investments, so that they understand everything about where their money is being placed. We do this through monthly educational events both online and in person, rather than simply relying on annual or quarterly reviews. This education is largely responsible for the happy fact that we've lost very few clients during the several recent economic crises, and we think this says something about our service and our clients' results. If you asked a thousand investment advisers if they've lost any clients over the past two tumultuous years, very few could say they haven't.

By this point, you're probably thinking: what is so different about the way we teach our clients to invest?

Let's return briefly to the 2008 crash. As you know, it wasn't just the stock market that suffered, it was also the banks; and because the banks were suffering, they stopped lending. What this did was open up an entire new marketplace for private lending opportunities high-quality, high-return to solid companies that suddenly couldn't get their hands on any capital. We consider this to be a completely non-correlated asset; in other words, what the market does on any given day does not affect the performance of this type of asset.

A few years ago, banks would finance deals at 5% interest, and sometimes fund them all the way to 100%, without thinking twice. Now they won't even think twice about approving much smaller loans, which has locked out entire industries from having access to critical funds that they wouldn't have had a problem obtaining before the crash. (Let's remember, it was home mortgages that caused the meltdown, not this kind of business loans.)

Here's a good example of what I'm talking about. I hold an equity partnership in an alternative energy company. The reason I have this partnership is that this particular company was scheduled to be funded in December 2008 with $30 million by a hedge fund that was capitalized by one of the large investment banks. When Lehman Brothers went down in November 2008, it had a ripple effect through the lending world and this alternative energy company was abruptly left out in the cold. It was a completely valid and bankable deal, but all of a sudden, Lehman was no longer in business and no one else was lending.

This company then had to waste another year and a half trying to get the capital required to move forward. They had everything they needed to succeed—contracts in place, a solid business model, a management team with the necessary experience—except the cash to get to the next level.

This was a quality deal that we could take advantage of if the banks wouldn't. In the past, we would have had to manufacture the deal from the ground up. It would have required a great deal of due diligence, putting together the right team to run the company, and creating the right business model to make sure it could succeed. Now, however, great management teams running quality companies are knocking on our door to get access to capital. The banks' loss is our investors' gain.

One of the investors I'm talking about is a good friend of mine who has a degree from the London School of Economics and speaks at Harvard Business School. He's experienced such high returns from these kinds of investments that he's always on the lookout for more deals of this sort. He feels that right now, America is basically "on sale" : we've never seen a period in our history where you could access these kinds of opportunities and get monster returns in many cases.

I couldn't agree more. That's why my rallying cry is that we should revolutionize the way financial products are created and sold, putting the control back into the hands of investors rather than the grip of the big institutions. It sure beats going down to your local financial advisers' office and trusting that one of its employees is going to get you any kind of return—because he's not.

APPROACHING ALTERNATIVE INVESTMENTS

My biggest piece of advice for anyone interested in trying these kinds of investments is to educate yourself. That education begins with networking and building relationships with people who are actually doing it. There are a lot of so-called experts out there, selling how-to books and other products, but these aren't the people to work with. You should invest with people actually participating in these investments, not those whose profit depends on selling you information about them.

Another important consideration with financial investments (or really with any kind of investment) is to focus not only on the return or the risk. Instead, consider your comprehensive investment strategy and how this particular investment fits into it. Think about the reason you're getting into a given investment, what you'll do if you benefit from it, and how it might affect you if it doesn't work out. To me, the investment strategy is a crucial element of the process and the single biggest reason for the success or failure of a portfolio, whether that portfolio contains stocks, bonds, real estate, or other investments like the ones we're discussing here.

Finally, look at your mindset when you're considering an investment. A successful investor does not base his or her decisions on fear; instead, he or she accepts the concept of abundance. If you're making a call based solely on fear, it's already the wrong one. Fear has nothing to do with facts, and it prevents you from seeing clearly. Unfortunately, money inspires that kind of fear too often. The great investors, however, triumph over this kind of negative emotion.

Again, If you're interested in having access to real information about these kinds of investments, try to avoid people who are marketing either informational products or in-person seminars to you. They are probably the wrong kind of advisers to use. The very best investment people in this new financial world are hard to find and even harder to access. The others are the ones who don't have a solid record of achievement in this world.

Yes, it's a bit of a Catch-22: you should work with people who don't need the business, but because they don't need the business, they probably won't work with you. However, I may be able to help you network within this exclusive circle. Feel free to email me at corbincowan@me.com to discuss your objectives, and I can try and match you up with the right people.

And please, don't believe all the downbeat financial news: this is actually one of the most exciting times to invest in recent history. Opportunities are everywhere—just look for the right one to hold onto, and find a coach who will keep you disciplined!

About Corbin

Corbin Cowan: Bringing Peace of Mind to Main Street Investors

In the world of financial advisers and experts, few have the hands-on finance and business experience backing their training that Corbin Cowan brings to his clients. After building, owning and managing several successful businesses in financial services, the oil and gas industry, and real estate and property management, raising $150 million in funding commitments, Corbin has a unique perspective from his own personal successes and failures. His insights come from his extensive professional training balanced by real world experiences. This allows him to guide you through some of your most important decisions regarding your financial goals and investment choices and your family's financial security.

Even while he was earning his bachelor's degree in Finance from the University of Colorado, he founded Rocky Mountain Investment Management, LLC, which was funded and managed by student shareholders. After he graduated, Corbin became President of C & J Exploration, overseeing their strategic planning, establishing their business structure, providing financial and economic evaluation, negotiating and implementing partnership agreements and joint venture opportunities, among many other responsibilities.

Working with wealthy investors and funding groups to secure growth capital, he realized that the old adage "The rich get richer" had a foundation in fact: Millionaires get billionaire opportunities, but wealthy individuals have always known that the planning process itself is more important than any individual investment. The process of planning long-term strategies effectively requires looking at all aspects of a client's portfolio, including his or her goals, values and timelines. The wealthy have long enjoyed the help of "family offices" employing financial, legal, accounting and estate planning experts, to guide their financial decisions. Unfortunately, these services can cost hundreds of thousands of dollars a year. This is not a problem if you are a multi-millionaire, celebrity or NFL player.

This severely limits the average investor's options to commissioned salespeople: stockbrokers, insurance agents, and others. They earn their by selling their firm's in-house financial products. This creates an inherent conflict of interest, yet most average investors have been schooled to look at products first, strategies later (if at all).

Corbin realized that to give average investors the kind of advantages the super-wealthy enjoy, it would take more than just presenting the right "opportunities." Only by providing normal hard-working individuals access to the highest level of financial education, would he enable Main Street investors to realize the kind of peace of mind about their investments that the wealthy have always known.

You owe it to yourself and your family to get in touch with Corbin today at corbincowan@me.com, and to find out what a difference coaching will make in your life.

CHAPTER 11

Cashing in on the Foreclosure Crisis: Buying and Flipping Bank-Owned Properties

By Nancy Geils

Hello, and welcome to the chapter on buying and flipping real estate-owned properties, or REOs. I'm so excited that you're here. In this chapter, you'll learn a multitude of tips for and secrets to buying foreclosed properties from the banks.

When we first started investing in real estate 12 years ago, my husband had just closed a business he and his father had been running. After spending 9 years as a marketing specialist for a corporation, I had just been laid off, and after waiting years to conceive, I was pregnant with our first child!

With neither of us employed and a baby on the way, I was scared and losing sleep. One night, I was up late watching TV and saw a late-night real estate infomercial. I got excited and bought the program! The next day, I purchased the book "Nothing Down" by Robert G. Allen, and I read it again and again, cover to cover, realizing that I too could do this. My husband and I then decided that our first strategy would be to buy multi-family units for the cash flow. We found our first deal and put down a deposit. Then suddenly, reality set in and we panicked. Have you ever felt the same way? Have you ever started out on a new adventure but then been paralyzed by the fear of jumping in?

We decided together that we didn't know enough about real estate and that we didn't want to buy the house, and the next day we marched down to our attorney's office to tell him that we'd made a big mistake and that we wanted out. He advised us that if we backed out of this deal, we would lose our $3000 deposit. As we were out of work and starting a family, we could not afford to lose that money.

We went home feeling confused and scared, but decided to bite the bullet and move forward. Every day, I thank God for the situation we'd found ourselves in. If we hadn't been told that we would lose our deposit, we would have never have gotten started in real estate in the first place. The moral of my story is that the first deal is the hardest, but once you make it and begin collecting the extra profit after expenses, your fears will subside. After the first deal, each one becomes "just another deal"!

Here it is: our first multi-family unit. It's not the best-looking house, but the cash flow was great and it was fully rented!

In this chapter, I'll show you how to make quick cash by buying and flipping bank-owned properties, or REOs, which are properties that go back to the lender after the foreclosure auction takes place. You should note that my book isn't just for beginners; however, I frequently reference beginners because often they are the investors who need the most help finding properties and money. But if you're a seasoned professional who's looking for ideas and advice on how to improve your cash flow, you should also listen up.

Whether you're a novice or an expert, no matter where you are in the timeline of real estate investing, what you'll learn about and develop here are skills that apply to everyone.

TESTIMONIAL

"Nancy is one of the coolest coaches you can have to guide and teach you the roads of success in Real Estate Wholesaling. You can definitely count on her being there for you—she always answered the phone when I called her for a quick question or when I felt I was stuck with an obstacle. You get to speak with her directly, which I find awesome. I felt like I wasn't left alone with a bunch of books and tapes to try and figure out what to do next. The support alone that you get from her is worth every single penny you invest in her training." -C. Giddens

Buying and Flipping REOs for Quick Cash Profit

The banks are selling these houses so cheaply—for literally pennies on the dollar. You see, they've already made their money off of the American people. And they made even more with the passage of the $787 billion stimulus bill in 2009.

As of today—right now—this opportunity still exists, and I call it the "Gold Rush."

REOs are some of the best deals around!

To get insider information on the REOs available in your target market, you will need to network with bankers, lenders and real estate agents in your area.

Introducing My Six-Step Formula For Buying And Selling REOs!

These are the ingredients that make for real estate success:

5%: tips, techniques, strategies and education

15%: money management skills

80%: psychology and emotion

There's a perfect storm brewing out there for bank-owned properties. They are arriving on the market in droves. It's an unfortunate situation for the people who are losing their homes, but for real estate investors it's the greatest market I've seen in years. There are several factors making this a great time to be a real estate investor: huge numbers of foreclosures, lots of people needing homes, the disappearance of most of the competition, and extremely low interest rates for first-time home buyers.

THE SIX-STEP FORMULA

Step 1: Build Your Cash Buyers List

The first and most important step is to create your cash buyers list. You must have this list in hand well before you find your first bank-owned property deal. These cash investors will hopefully be repeat buyers for you! Strive to find for as many buyers as you can.

Advertising is a great way to find them! You can start building your cash buyers list by putting ads on Craigslist (which is free) and in the local newspaper. Here's one of the sample ads that I put up on Craigslist:

- Handyman Special
- Worth $110K, Will Sell $55
- Call for details: 203-555-1212

Step 2: Find the Best Deals

You can buy bank-owned properties or short sales.

Here are a few good sites for finding deals, and of course realtors will still be your best source for locating them:

- www.gohoming.com
- www.econohomes.com
- www.hudhomestore.com
- www.homepath.com

It's easy to find an REO Broker. Google REO Brokers in your town or try www.REOBroker.com. Just type in your town and zip code. Tell them you are a cash buyer. Usually brokers have what they call a "hot list," and they will send you a daily list of every new foreclosure property that comes up. **Tip:** Look for the properties that have come back on the market.

Step 3: Find Funding and Use One-Day Funding

You can do an internet search to find companies that offer one-day funding—there are many out there who do so. These companies will provide one-day funding for your deals and they are also known as transactional funding lenders. They wire in the money and the ONLY requirement is that you have a cash buyer under contract, lined up and ready to go!

Some Pitfalls to Avoid:

Mistake #1: Not Having Buyers Ready to Go
If you find a good deal but you don't have a buyer, your deal will fall through. Build your list of buyers first!

Mistake #2: Offering Too Much Money for the Property

Mistake #3: Not Knowing the REAL Value of the Property.
Make sure to use your realtors, since they know the market in a given area. They'll be glad to help you.

Step 4: What to Look for When Your Realtor Tells You about a Great Deal

Here are EZ Quick indicators of a house's condition:

1. Age or condition of the roof

2. Presence of central heating and central air conditioning

3. How recently the kitchen and baths were updated

My First REO Deal

Here is a recent deal I've done:

- Negotiated house purchase and got it under contract from the bank for $72,000

- House needed about $30,000 in rehab

- Post-repair value was $170,000

- Found my cash investor buyer and signed the Purchase and Sale Agreement

- My buyer still made a huge profit: approximately $50,000

- And my profit was $10,000!

Why Wouldn't New Investor Buyers Make an Offer by Themselves?

- Your cash buyers are not going to buy these flips. They are too busy rehabbing. They're out there fixing properties. They are managing their contractors. They are fixing houses and selling them. They don't have time to sit in front of a computer and talk to realtors to make sure they're getting a good deal.

Step 5: Getting Your REO Under Contract with a Cash Buyer

You are now getting close to collecting your wholesale fee! You've found and negotiated an REO property and have it under contract with the bank. You now have to call all the cash buyers you've already lined up and tell them about your deal. Bring them to the property to show it to them. Remember: they're buying in as-is condition. If they want the property, have them sign a contract with you and then get ready to close the deal!

Step 6: Closing the Deal and Collecting Your Wholesale Fee
Congratulations: you've made it to the final step in buying and flipping REOs! Now is the time to get your one-day funding lined up and ready to go—unless you are using your own cash, of course. Contact your attorney or title company and close the deal. You will buy with one-day funding, sell on the same day to your cash buyer, and collect your check!

What Should Your Wholesaling Fee Be? Depending on how good the deal is, you can set your fee at any amount you wish. My highest was $20,000, but if you get a really cheap deal, you can make even more money. The norm is $2,000 to $10,000.

You have now completed the six-step formula "How to Wholesale Bank-Owned Properties." As you can see, this strategy is a simple one for making quick cash, but you must follow the steps one by one!

In conclusion, buying and flipping bank-owned properties is the easiest way to get started in real estate investing if you are short on cash or new at the game. It is one of the best "New Rules Of The Game"! Good luck and happy investing! If you would like more information about me and my courses, or to have me speak at one of your events, please contact me at my office 800-804-5390.

Nancy Geils
P.O. Box 11
Monroe, CT 06468
800-804-5390

For more information on Investing in Real Estate, or to enroll in my courses, you can visit:
www.REOBootcampTraining.com
www.InvestingwiththeStars.net/Season3 - Free Weekly Training
www.Linkedin.com/nancygeils
www.facebook.com/nancygeils

To join my Personal Coaching Program, visit:
www.WhyInvestInRealEstate.com
www.realestateinvestingnewsletter.com

About Nancy

Nancy Geils has quickly established herself as a respected expert in the fields of real estate investing, wholesaling and coaching. With her enduring enthusiasm for the business and recent hands-on experience in structuring and closing deals, she has brought a breath of fresh air into the world of real estate education. She has been called the "coolest coach" in real estate investing because she really cares.

Nancy applies and grows her knowledge daily in her company and then shares these groundbreaking techniques with her students. The results are evident: In the past three years alone, her real estate investing company Home Solutions Group, LLC has purchased, rehabbed and wholesaled more than 100 single-family homes, and it owns and controls many multi-family apartment buildings. She has bought over $25 million worth of real estate deals and investments within the last decade.

To learn more about Nancy Geils, and how you can receive her free special report titled, "Your Income Explosion Guide to Making Money in Real Estate: Seven Powerful Reasons Why You Should Be Investing In Real Estate In Today's Market," visit www.nancygeils.com.

Testimonials:

"Nancy is amazing. She is part of my personal mastermind and I have enjoyed learning her vast experience in the foreclosure arena!"
—Robert G. Allen, Owner, Enlightened Wealth Institute

"Nancy is a brilliant real estate investor and teacher of real estate investing and mentor to many successful real estate investors. I have known Nancy for several years and can only recommend to anyone interested in real estate investing to work with her."
—Jack Bosch, Managing Director, Orbit Publishing, LLC

CHAPTER 12

Network Marketing: "It's Just One of Those Things"

By Jill Picerno

Most people do not truly understand what network marketing is, but many of them will tell you that it is bad. If you ask them to explain why they feel that way, they might say, "It's just one of those things." Yes, network marketing is just one of those things. It is a different type of business model that most people do not understand. If you actually take the time to listen to very successful entrepreneurs, they will share with you that network marketing is the best business model out there if you want to become financially free. It is worth taking the time to understand how it all works. Network Marketing is truly not a bad thing.

Learning about network marketing can be a ton of fun! You can learn about it through the Internet or by reading books, but the best way to learn is at the live training events that the network marketing company offers you. When you begin your journey, you should go to every training event possible. My career in network marketing began a little over four years ago, and I have attended so many training events that I've lost track of the number. These training events are not like the dry boring corporate business events that you may have attended in the past. The culture is so different. Imagine being surrounded by a bunch of positive, upbeat friends who enjoy life to the fullest while you learn how to be a better you! Yes, our training sessions actually help you learn more about yourself than about the techniques of our business.

Most network marketing companies, I believe, are really personal development companies in disguise. You will be tested and challenged in so many different ways! You will learn how to do this business, but you will also definitely learn how to get yourself out of your comfort zone to excel here. You will be paid for your performance and not by the hour for your time. It's a different type of business model, one in which you have control of your destiny. We are all not born network marketers, but we can all become network marketers. Learning about network marketing can be one of the best things you can do for yourself and your family, while creating a ton of fun on your journey to freedom.

So here's my story. Before you read any farther, I want you to know that I haven't made it all the way to the top yet with my network marketing business, but I will. I hope my story will help you have an easier time than I did getting to where I am now. However, make no mistake; you will have struggles along the way. We all do, but they are worth it!

A little over four years ago, I was introduced to my current network marketing company, the one I joined and have stayed with. I'm always open to new opportunities, as I think we all should be, because we don't really know what we don't really know, until we actually take the time to listen with a nonjudgmental mindset. I was in my family room with a friend of mine when I first learned about the company. A couple of her friends came over and proceeded to show us a video about their network marketing company. I knew I was going to join even before their video ended, as it related to one of my passions, travel.

So my friend and I both jumped right in and bought a business position together. I had to live and learn that you should always buy your own business position. We are all different people with different values and work ethics. It is rare that a business position partnership in a network marketing company works out for any length of time. So just buy your own.

I was so excited about our new business that I was off and running.

Running my mouth, that is, to all my close friends and family about the incredible business I just found out about. Telling them that we were all going to be in business together and travel the world! I had no actual clue how to share my business with anyone. My word of advice is to keep quiet until you have a little training. I knew I really didn't know what I was doing, but I was so excited and thought that I could tell my close friends and family about this business and that they'd all jump right in with me. Boy, was I wrong. My friends and family didn't see what I saw, because they literally hadn't seen what I saw—the video presentation. When you open your mouth to your friends and family too early, they will make a judgment about the company and may resist taking a look at the actual video presentation for you in the future. Please learn from my mistake. I suggest you get at least some training before you begin to share your business with anyone.

So, after falling on my face many, many times with my new business, I decided to attend as many of the training sessions as I could. While I was going to all of these, the trainers suggested that I should listen to positive personal development CDs in my car and at home and start reading all the personal development books they recommended. I spent a lot of time and money doing this, but it has been worth it. I wasn't who I needed to be to have a successful network marketing business when I first joined. I needed training and still continue to do it today. For some reason, it seems that people who join network marketing companies think that they can just do this business on their own, without any training, and get great results. We all need training in any other career, so why do we think we know how to do this business, without it? Network marketing is a different type of business, as I've already mentioned. You need to learn the correct steps to take to move forward. Go to all the training programs you can, listen to positive personal development CDs in your car, and read all the personal development books they suggest. You will be amazed how this will change your life!

I have been so fortunate to have been trained by some of the best of the best network marketers in the business! I've learned everything I know from them! There is so much information I would like to share with you here, but my space is limited. I still believe, though, that my top five new rules of the network marketing game can be game changers for you.

First, you have to have your "why" ("Why am I doing this?") written down in detail on paper with a deadline for completion! This is huge! It sounds simple, but the majority of people in network marketing never complete this step. You have to know why you are willing to get out of your comfort zone and press on. It's hard to pursue your why, your dreams, your goals, when you don't know what they really are and when you desire to achieve them. This may be a little harsh, but I believe it is necessary to prove this point. When you are lying on your deathbed, wouldn't it be great to be able to say "I did it and have no regrets!" instead of, "I wish I did, but now there is no time left." What is your "why"? What would make your life all it can be, according to you, without any regrets at the end? This is for only you to decide. Take some quiet time by yourself with pen and paper in your hand and think this through now. What would help you press on when you run into dream stealers? Dream stealers are people, most likely those very close to you, who think they are helping or saving you when they say "network marketing is bad, it's a scam, it's a pyramid," and so on. I was taught to listen to successful people. If you are going to listen to the dream stealers, than you must be willing to live their lifestyle—otherwise, why would you listen to them in the first place? Listen and learn from the people who have the lifestyle that looks like your own "why." Who has accomplished some of your own dreams or your goals? Look at and duplicate what they have done, so you can reach your "why." Knowing your "why" will put you on the path to your success.

Second, you have to be willing to invest some time and money into your personal development and training. No one gets to the top without going through this process. You will learn about inviting (the right way), duplication (with the use of tools), telling stories not facts (as facts tell and stories sell), leverage (using other people's time), team dynamics (personal interactions), your product (its advantages), and more. Plus using your product is a requirement, as this is part of your training as well. How can you sell something you don't use? Be prepared to spend some time learning about yourself and your new business to progress forward. You will also have to spend more money than just the original outlay for your business center and products. All businesses require additional funds. However, the amount of money you will need to spend is nowhere near what it would cost to buy your own franchise. So be prepared to allot some time to this business and some additional money as well. Your rewards will be worth the sacrifice.

Third, realize that you now need to consider how to use social media to increase your sales in your business. You should create account profiles on all of the social media sites that are currently active, and that your prospects will be using. Be aware of how you are branding yourself when you create your account profiles. We all have some type of brand presence on the Internet, and you need to be aware of how you are being perceived. There are so many things to learn about all the various social media sites, all of which are changing so rapidly, that it may be easier to pay someone to help you set up and maintain your social media accounts. Your time can be better spent on money-making activities for your business. Also, when your social media accounts are up and running, be aware that spamming is not an acceptable practice. The website owners can actually delete your account profile and block you from using their website if you are caught spamming. So, what do you do? You become active, from a purely social perspective, on all of these sites. Then, every five or so posts you just hint about your network marketing business or the incredible lifestyle that you have created for yourself and your family from your business. Remember— only hint about these things. You don't want to give away all of your information at once for free, without controlling who sees what and when they see it. Hints get people's curiosity aroused, and that's a good thing in network marketing. So: become socially active on the Internet, but don't give away your information by spamming everyone.

Fourth, remember that even though we are becoming an Internet-based and texting society, the best way to share your business with someone is still face-to-face. You can use the Internet and text messages to send some of your invites, but if at all possible, you should meet with your prospects in person when sharing your business with them. Over 50% of our communication is related to our body language. Only a very small percentage of our actual words help relay what we are actually trying to communicate. When some people start their network marketing careers, they are always searching for the exact words to say when presenting the business opportunity so that their prospects get involved. However, there are no exact words. I believe that you can't say the right thing to the wrong prospect or the wrong thing to the right prospect. Body language and the tone of your voice, which relates to your excitement level, are actually what helps you make more sales than the words you are using during your presentation. If you are not with your prospect when you are sharing your business with them, you are at a huge disadvantage. Therefore, you should always strive to meet with your prospects in person when sharing your network marketing business opportunity with them.

The **fifth** and final new rule to the game of network marketing is not really new at all, but without it, you can't really succeed. You need to do something—meaning a money-making activity—towards your network marketing career goals and dreams every single day! Money-making activities involve contacting and meeting with your prospects in person, if at all possible. Remember your first rule is to figure out your "why." In the fifth rule, you need to write down the steps that you need to be working on daily to reach your dreams and goals, which need to include money-making activities. Start writing these steps out on paper with deadlines next to them. Then start working towards your "why"! Make your plan and stick to it.

So let's try and put this all into perspective. Network marketing is really not bad at all. It is an awesome career that you can have for yourself, but realize that not everyone will understand what you do or why you do it. Know that there are certain steps that you need to take to make this a profitable business for yourself and your family. You really need to know **why** you are doing this! This is a huge key to your success. I am so glad I decided to take the path less traveled.

About Jill

Jill Nieman Picerno is a network marketer! One of her major "whys" is that she wants to continue to be a stay-at-home mom for her teenage daughters, and later in her life travel the world with them when they have their own families. She enjoys creating memories that will last beyond a lifetime—to her, creating incredible memories is what life is all about! She also wants her girls to have total financial freedom and time flexibility in the future, which her business can create for them. She owns a network marketing travel business, in which she loves helping other people realize their dreams. She is rewarded when she watches them grow from who they were to who they become after they make their personal development and network marketing training a high priority in their lives. Jill has always had an entrepreneurial spirit. She went to school and became a Certified Public Accountant so that she could run her own business out of her home when she had little ones to care for. Being a stay-at-home mom has always been one of her goals in life, and she's proud that she was able to accomplish this and continues to do so today. She loves network marketing, as it allows her to spend time with her girls, to be learning new things all the time, to be around positive, upbeat people and to be able to visit new places around the world. She knows that she is a very lucky lady!

Jill Nieman Picerno
10940 S. Parker Rd, Ste. 472
Parker, CO 80134
303-400-5100
jill@travelgirls.biz
www.Dreamories.com

"Where Dreams Become Memories"

CHAPTER 13

THE NEW RULES FOR BECOMING AN AUTHOR: THE SIX MYTHS OF PUBLISHING SUCCESS

By Nick Nanton, JW Dicks, Lindsay Dicks & Greg Rollett

At the age of 26, Amanda Hocking was an unpublished writer living in Minnesota who had written 17 novels. But no big publisher wanted any part of her. So, while she worked at her $18,000-a-year job, she decided to take things into her own hands—and worked with a small publishing company to make her books available for sale on Amazon.

Two years later, she had made millions from her e-book sales—and also struck a multi-million dollar book deal with the well-established publisher St. Martin's Press.

That's not how book deals used to happen. But the internet has changed our world to such an extent that it's naive to think that book publishing wouldn't be included in this tremendous transformation. Hocking's story will continue to be duplicated in years to come.

At the Dicks + Nanton Celebrity Branding® Agency, we believe in the new publishing paradigm that has emerged, and we enjoy leveraging it on behalf of our clients. You're reading one of the happy results of these efforts right at this moment!

Still, there are many misconceptions that people have about what publishing is all about—and just what they need (or don't need) to do to get a book published. We'd like to dispel all the misinformation we've seen in our extensive combined experience in publishing over the past three decades, and give you the lowdown on "The 6 Myths of Publishing Success."

MYTH #1: I JUST NEED TO FIND THE RIGHT AGENT FOR MY BOOK.

Would-be writers used to face the same Catch-22 as would-be actors, singers and screenplay writers—they couldn't break into the business without the right agent, but no agent would take them seriously unless they were already in the business!

Conventional old-school publishers have never paid a great deal of attention to a manuscript submitted by an unknown. That's why book agents came into being—they were reputable people trusted by publishing companies who could recognize talent and direct it their way.

But, again, it was hard to get an agent's attention if you had no track record. You had to send them a proposal with some sample chapters, wait a few months for a reply, and then start the process all over again with another agent. It's generally against protocol to send the same book to several agents at once, so it could literally take years before you got an agent—if you got one at all. And then that agent had to try and find your book a publisher, which is another lengthy, drawn-out process.

Nobody has to endure those long delays anymore. Just as a singer like Lana Del Rey can get herself booked on "Saturday Night Live" through her YouTube videos, you can get yourself published in record time these days without ever talking to an agent.

MYTH #2: I SHOULD BE PAID TO WRITE MY BOOK.

We're all used to getting money for what we do, so you might quite reasonably expect a publisher to give you a nice advance to write your book. Well, the unfortunate truth is that unless you are already an established author, it's more likely than not that you're not going to get an advance. Many established authors even have difficulty getting them these days, as a matter of fact. In fact, just the other day, we were reviewing a publishing agreement for someone who is literally a household name, one of the biggest personalities in sports, and his publishing advance was all of four figures. Yup, a few grand! Believe me when I tell you that his is a BIG name.

Instead of looking at it as a payday, you should think about your book as a marketing opportunity for yourself and/or your business. Don't get us wrong—you can and should make money from having a book—but you'll find most people don't make that money from actually selling the book. The great news is that there are tons of other ways to make money from your book, just not in the ways people usually imagine. Your profits will most likely come not from big sales (although we certainly won't tell you that can't happen), but rather from how the book boosts your brand and opens doors for you, which we'll discuss a little later. As we like to say, "A book can take you places you could never take yourself!"

MYTH #3: I NEED A HUGE NEW YORK PUBLISHER LIKE RANDOM HOUSE OR SIMON & SCHUSTER.

You might think your book won't be credible unless you have a behemoth New York publisher on board to back it—you know, one of the ones that's been around since the 1800s or so. You might think that they excel at marketing and promotion and that they'll give your book the push it needs to go straight to the top.

Well, our experience, as well as the experience of countless other clients and friends of ours (including those who have sold literally millions of books) wouldn't bear out that assertion. Again, the publishing world has drastically changed, and the traditional publishers really only work with books that pretty much sell themselves. Of course, the latest Donald Trump business book and Stephen King thriller will be printed by one of the big boys. They jump after books that are all-but-guaranteed best-sellers.

As Amanda Hocking would tell you, what they're not very interested in is an unpublished novice writer who lacks a very well-known name or a huge media platform. They aren't looking for anything they can't "pre-sell," unless it comes with a magnificent literary pedigree or the author is a recognized journalist with some big scoop. The established publishers (and agents for that matter) *want the easiest sale they can make*, as they want to avoid having to spend millions to promote an unknown quantity who may or may not make a dent on the best-seller lists.

And let's talk about marketing. Basically, if you are successful in convincing an agent or a publisher to back your book, it's because you've told them how well you can market it in your book proposal. So what do you need them for? It's much better to work with a publishing operation that understands this, and your goals for your book—which should be to build your platform, your business and your income. This kind of business will not only put your marketing ideas into the mix, but also add some sizzle of its own. If you know why your book has appeal, you have the most important tool you need to get out there and make a splash yourself—and you won't end up caught in the gears at a major publishing house that can't change marketing strategies on a dime like you can!

Here's the bottom line. It used to be that, in order to sell a song, a book, a movie, or any other creative work, you were forced to impress what we call "an audience of one." In other words, before you could get your work out to the public, you had to go through an individual gate-keeper—an agent, a publisher, or some other kind of decision-maker who, like the ancient Roman emperors, could give your endeavor the rare thumbs-up or the all-too-common and deadly thumbs-down.

The new model of publishing has blown up that myth, and now allows you to control your own destiny.

MYTH #4: I NEED TO WRITE EVERY WORD OF MY BOOK MYSELF.

Many a would-be author spends hours staring at a blank Worddocument on his or her computer screen. And staring...and staring...

He or she figures, "It's *my* book. I have to write it."

The truth is that just *organizing* the contents of a book is an art—and if you've never had any experience with putting together a book, you'll likely find yourself going around in circles. Imagine trying to put a car engine together without first knowing anything about cars. Trying to write your first book is not that far off.

That's why ghostwriters get work—and are hired by some of the top names out there. James Patterson is able to release as many thrillers as he does because he uses a whole number of co-writers. Tom Clancy ("The Hunt for Red October") uses them, too. And you can bet that almost every celebrity publishing his or her "autobiography" uses one. Professional ghostwriters can be trusted to deliver a professional product that reads like *you* wrote it.

That's because you don't just say to a ghostwriter, "Hey, write a book for me," and then wait for the manuscript to show up. (Well, you can, but don't be surprised if you don't like the result!) No, a good ghostwriter will get the appropriate content from you, either through notes or phone interviews, and then write the book in your specific "voice," so that the book sounds like you and expresses what it is you want it to say. It's the best— and fastest—route to a finished, professional book.

Remember what staring at a blank page did to Jack Nicholson in "The Shining"? You don't need that in your life!

MYTH #5: IT WILL TAKE YEARS TO WRITE AND SELL MY BOOK.

If you stick to the traditional publishing methods, you can already see how Myth #5 could be oh-so-true. Writing the book yourself could take more than a year. Then it could take you another year or so just to get an agent. And *then*, it could take another year or so until the agent got you a publisher. Oh, and you're not out of the woods yet. The publisher will assign the book to an editor, who will probably have you revise the book, which will take a few more months.

And then...they finally have to schedule a *release date* on their publishing calendar. Which means they have to work your book in around all their other titles?

Which means whatever you wrote will already be five years out of date by the time anybody has a chance to read it!

There are ways to jump-start this whole process and get it done in a reasonable amount of time. If you're not a fast or experienced writer, a ghostwriter will help you get the book finished quickly. If you work with a smaller, cutting-edge publishing company that knows how to market your book in the 21st century, you'll be able to get it out on the market in no time. The old way is fraught with bureaucracy; the new way is all about getting the best results in the shortest possible time period.

MYTH #6: I WILL MAKE MONEY FROM BOOK SALES.

Every author dreams of his or her book becoming a smash success, and people scooping it up in droves at bookstores across the country.

Well, besides the fact that almost every bookstore across the country is either out of business or headed in that direction, this is a fantasy that almost never happens with books, especially when they're by authors who haven't already sold millions of books. There certainly are exceptions, but, more often than not, books aren't big money-makers—even when they're written by extraordinary people.

If you're writing a book because you think you will make money on sales, of either electronic downloads or physical hardcovers or paperbacks, think again. You probably won't and, if you do, it probably won't add up to much.

The real pay-off for writing a book is with your brand and the growth of your business, as we mentioned earlier. You see an immediate and tremendous rise in your profile when you become a published author. You also have a great tool for publicity, since it's easier to book speaking engagements or media appearances with a book on your résumé.

Most of all, it's amazing for business. One of our clients, Brian Horn, nailed down a huge multi-million dollar business deal, just because he was able to pull out a copy of his current best-selling book, which featured *his* picture on the cover. The client was impressed not only because Brian had this achievement under his belt, but also because the client could tell his clients that the project was being supervised by a best-selling author!

As you can see, publishing is a completely different animal in the 21st century. But don't just take our word for it. Read the following words from former literary agent and author Nathan Bransford (and remember, he's a professional who has worked in old-school publishing):

"I think the big problem with traditional publishing is they seem dead-set on making themselves irrelevant....more and more we're being told that publishers don't have time to edit books. We have to self-edit before sending them in.

Brick-and-mortar stores are going away. The marketing budget of a book basically goes entirely into store placement (and maybe not for your book)....advances are getting smaller and smaller....it's rapidly becoming a bad deal for authors who are not automatic best-sellers."

The facts are undeniable. If you want to make a book happen, do it on your own or with the help of a publisher who understands how today's publishing marketplace really works.

You'll be glad you did.

About Nick

An Emmy-winning director and producer, Nick Nanton, Esq., is known as the top agent to celebrity experts around the world for his role in developing and marketing business and professional experts through personal branding, media, marketing and PR to help them gain credibility and recognition for their accomplishments. Nick is recognized as the nation's leading expert on personal branding as *Fast Company* magazine's expert blogger on the subject and lectures regularly on the topic at major universities around the world. His book "Celebrity Branding You" has also been used as the textbook on personal branding for university students.

The CEO of The Dicks + Nanton Celebrity Branding Agency, an international agency with more than 1000 clients in 26 countries, Nick is an award-winning director, producer and songwriter who has worked on everything from large-scale events to television shows with Bill Cosby, President George H.W. Bush, Brian Tracy, Michael Gerber and many more.

Nick is recognized as one of the top thought leaders in the business world and has co-authored 16 best-selling books alongside Brian Tracy, Jack Canfield (creator of the "Chicken Soup for the Soul" series), Dan Kennedy, Robert Allen, Dr. Ivan Misner (founder of BNI), Jay Conrad Levinson (author of the "Guerilla Marketing" series), Leigh Steinberg and many others, including the breakthrough hit "Celebrity Branding You!"

Nick has led the marketing and PR campaigns that have driven more than 600 authors to best-seller status. Nick has been seen in *USA Today, The Wall Street Journal, Newsweek, Inc., The New York Times, Entrepreneur Magazine* and FastCompany.com and has appeared on ABC, NBC, CBS, and FOX television affiliates around the country, as well as on FOX News, CNN, CNBC and MSNBC, speaking on subjects ranging from branding, marketing and law to "American Idol."

Nick is a member of the Florida Bar and holds a J.D. from the University of Florida Levin College of Law, as well as a B.S./B.A. in Finance from the University of Florida's Warrington College of Business Administration. Nick is a voting member of The National Academy of Recording Arts & Sciences

(NARAS, home to the Grammys), a member of The National Academy of Television Arts & Sciences (home to the Emmy Awards), co-founder of the National Academy of Best-Selling Authors, and an 11-time Telly Award winner. He spends his spare time working with Young Life and Downtown Credo Orlando and rooting for the Florida Gators with his wife Kristina and their three children, Brock, Bowen and Addison.

About JW

JW Dicks, Esq. is America's foremost authority on using personal branding for business development. He has created some of the most successful brand and marketing campaigns for business and professional clients to make them the credible celebrity experts in their field and build multi-million dollar businesses using their recognized status.

JW Dicks has started, bought, built, and sold a large number of businesses over his 39-year career and developed a loyal international following as a business attorney, author, speaker, consultant, and business experts' coach. He not only practices what he preaches by using his strategies to build his own businesses, he also applies those same concepts to help clients grow their business or professional practice the ways he does.

JW has been extensively quoted in such national media as *USA Today, The Wall Street Journal, Newsweek, Inc.*, Forbes.com, CNBC.com, and *Fortune Small Business*. His television appearances include ABC, NBC, CBS and FOX affiliate stations around the country. He is the resident branding expert for *Fast Company*'s internationally syndicated blog and is the publisher of *Celebrity Expert Insider*, a monthly newsletter targeting business and brand building strategies.

JW has written over 22 books, including numerous best-sellers, and has been inducted into the National Academy of Best-Selling Authors. JW is married to Linda, his wife of 39 years, and they have two daughters, two granddaughters and two Yorkies. JW is a 6th generation Floridian and splits his time between his home in Orlando and beach house on the Florida west coast.

About Lindsay

Lindsay Dicks helps her clients tell their stories in the online world. Having been brought up around a family of marketers, but a product of Generation Y, Lindsay naturally gravitated to the new world of online marketing. Lindsay began freelance writing in 2000 and soon after launched her own PR firm that thrived by offering an in-your-face "Guaranteed PR" that was one of the first of its kind in the nation.

Lindsay's new media career is centered on her philosophy that "people buy people." Her goal is to help her clients build a relationship with their prospects and customers. Once that relationship is built and they learn to trust them as the expert in their field, then they will do business with them. Lindsay also built a patent-pending process that utilizes social media marketing, content marketing and search engine optimization to create online "buzz" for her clients to helps them to convey their business and personal stories. Lindsay's clientele span the entire business map and range from doctors and small business owners to Inc. 500 CEOs.

Lindsay is a graduate of the University of Florida. She is the CEO of CelebritySites, an online marketing company specializing in social media and online personal branding. Lindsay is also a multi-best-selling author whose titles include the best-selling book "Power Principles for Success" which she co-authored with Brian Tracy. She was also selected as one of America's PremierExperts and has been quoted in *Newsweek*, the *Wall Street Journal*, *USA Today*, and *Inc.*, as well as featured on NBC, ABC, and CBS television affiliates speaking on social media, search engine optimization and making more money online. Lindsay was also recently brought on FOX 35 News as their online marketing expert.

Lindsay, a national speaker, has shared the stage with some of the top speakers in the world such as Brian Tracy, Lee Milteer, Ron LeGrand, Arielle Ford, David Bullock, Brian Horn, Peter Shankman and many others. Lindsay was also a producer on the Emmy-nominated film "Jacob's Turn."

You can connect with Lindsay at:
Lindsay@CelebritySites.com
www.twitter.com/LindsayMDicks
www.facebook.com/LindsayDicks

About Greg

Greg Rollett, the ProductPro, is a best-selling author and online marketing expert who works with authors, experts, entertainers, entrepreneurs and business owners all over the world to help them share their knowledge and change the lives and businesses of others. After creating a successful string of his own educational products, Greg began helping others in the production and marketing of their own products.

Greg is a front-runner in utilizing the power of social media, direct response marketing and customer education to drive new leads and convert those leads into long-standing customers and advocates.

Previous clients include Coca-Cola, Miller Lite, Warner Bros. and Cash Money Records, as well as hundreds of entrepreneurs and small-business owners. Greg's work has been featured on FOX News, ABC, and the Daily Buzz. Greg has written for Mashable, the Huffington Post, AOL, AMEX's Open Forum and more.

Greg loves to challenge the current business environments that constrain people to working 12-hour days during the best portions of their lives. By teaching them to leverage technology and the power of information, Greg loves helping others create freedom businesses that allow them to generate income, make the world a better place and live a radically ambitious lifestyle in the process.

A former touring musician, Greg is highly sought after as a speaker, having appeared on stages with former Florida Gov. Charlie Crist, best-selling authors Chris Brogan and Nick Nanton, and at events such as Affiliate Summit.

If you would like to learn more about Greg and how he can help your business, please contact him directly at greg@productprosystems.com or by calling his office at 877-897-4611.

You can also download a free report on how to create your own educational products at www.productprosystems.com.

CHAPTER 14

THE NEW RULES AND LAWS THAT GOVERN ALL HUMANS: The Secrets no one taught you about growing up to Achieve Success!

By Will Duquette

Do you want to make more money? Lose weight? Or stop smoking? If you answered yes to any of these questions, you will benefit from this chapter.

My name is Will "Power" Duquette. I now live in Jacksonville, Florida after years of moving around, searching for happiness and wealth. I grew up in a small town, with a childhood that I now realize was a very poor and difficult one, surrounded by negative people. Many people who grow up in this kind of environment seem to struggle with building massive wealth, having awesome relationships, and maintaining a healthy body. (I know, because I was one of them.) Maybe you're one of them, and you're now seeking to change your life. I applaud you for this and I promise that I will show you a better, more powerful way to live and transform those old programs that are keeping you from creating massive success. The one thing I ask is that YOU be open to change.

As you read, notice the **bold** phrases or affirmations. If you write them down and recite them daily, I guarantee that your life will begin to transform quickly. I know this information will create a massive shift in you, your finances, your relationships, and your happiness—it has for me! In my years of training and coaching, I have helped countless students achieve great success, and now it's your turn. No matter what it is you want to do, be, or have… you CAN do, be, or have… when you apply this powerful information.

I am a master hypnotist, and have performed countless stage hypnosis shows all around the world. I teach and train from many different sources, including the Bible, the law of attraction, the Universe, God, Conscious & subconscious mind, Hypnosis, or where ever. I do not tell people WHERE they should believe from, only that there are laws that govern all humans which have been scientifically proven. When these laws are learned and applied effectively, any human can achieve whatever they desire.

The number one thing I can teach you is that **in order for things to change, _you_ must change.** For most people, this is not good news, because we were taught from a very early age to resist change and not to take responsibility for our lives. But if you're overweight, and don't want to be, you must first change your exercise and eating habits. When students apply the laws I have taught them, it begins showing up in many areas throughout their life, such as weight loss. I've had many people report to me after losing anywhere from ten to 130 pounds in a very short amount of time and effectively keeping it off. It's really simple, folks: **eat less, move more!** And yet we have an overweight society due to old programs and old beliefs that do not serve us. Most of us were born into and grew up in what I call a pauper's mentality, instead of a millionaire's mentality. This is what keeps most people stuck in the vicious cycle of insanity, doing the same things over and over and expecting a different result. When I train people to become millionaires, this mentality spreads into all other areas of their lives. Once you've embedded all these laws in this chapter, all of this and more will happen easily–**because how you do anything is how you do everything!**

To better understand the mind, you must understand that you have two minds. Your conscious mind is the one that's aware and reading this book; it is the gatekeeper you use to judge and evaluate what you hear and see around you. The conscious mind is what most people use when they sit down to plan their goals for the future. But it has been scientifically proven that unless your subconscious mind is on board and reinforcing that those goals and dreams are possible, you will never attain them.

Your subconscious mind is like a computer. If you type a command into a computer, it immediately accepts the information and executes that command. If you or society embeds certain beliefs and programs into your subconscious mind, this "computer" starts performing exactly the way it's been programmed to work. Most of us have been programmed since birth to work hard, be humble, and not to talk to strangers. While adults know on a conscious level that it's okay to talk to strangers now, our subconscious still holds us back. I now tell my children, "Don't talk to strangers, until you're eighteen!"

How do you take charge of your own subconscious? It is programmed over time by any "I" or "I am" statements that you say. Words are so powerful that you must start by being very aware of what you say to yourself and to others. Many years ago, when I first uncovered this information, I decided that for 30 days I would simply respond "I'm great!" anytime someone asked me how I was. I committed to saying it as though it were true, although I had to fake it plenty of times. Within about two weeks, the most amazing thing happened: somebody asked me how I was, and I remember authentically feeling great for the first time in my life. So take on the same challenge for 30 days. The laws that govern you and all humans will transform your life, and after that you will be hooked on positive change and wanting more.

As you change the words you speak to others, they will start responding differently to you. You'll start to see more doors open and start attracting people towards you, rather than pushing them away. It might even seem a little spooky how effortlessly it happens. In order to maintain this new positive power, you must continue speaking about positive things that you want, and truly believe that you will attain them. Here are a few words to eliminate from your vocabulary: "try," "maybe," "hopefully," "problem," and any other negative words, especially when used with any "I" or "I am" statements. If you say, "I'm not confident," or "My problem is I'm (fill in the blank)," you embed these feelings in your subconscious and reinforce them. Start saying out loud what it is that you want to be: "**I am confident**," "**I believe in myself**," "**Others believe in me**," and so on. At first your brain may say, "No, you're not!" But I say, **Fake it 'til you make it.** Over time, you will reprogram your subconscious mind to believe you're confident, which will in turn make you more confident. Once you do it enough, it becomes effortless.

So far, I've taught you how to program yourself the right way in order to achieve your own personal goals. Now, I'm going to teach you how to block negative outside programming. When someone tells a story, he or she usually speaks in the second person: "You know when you're driving and someone pulls out in front of you cutting you off and it really makes you mad, so mad you just want to RAM your car right into them?" Now we all know consciously that the person telling the story is talking about themselves; the challenge is that your subconscious mind non-critically accepts all "you" statements. Let's look at the story again and I'll bold underline all the "YOU" programming. "**You** know when **you're** driving and someone pulls out in front of **you**, cutting **you** off and it really makes **you** mad, so mad **you** just want to RAM **your** car right into them?" In that story, there were seven examples of a direct embedded command on your subconscious mind. Your subconscious heard that you, not the speaker, got mad. And your subconscious is on 24/7. Some of you may be thinking, "How can I prevent all those people from programming me? Am I supposed to stop and correct them?" No, when I'm faced with this, I simply remind myself that they don't mean me. I block it out and you can too.

As I mentioned, my upbringing didn't serve to help me build wealth or to live powerfully. I worked hard, sometimes holding three jobs at once, but realized very quickly that was not how to achieve wealth. I went to college to learn how to become a millionaire and didn't. I tried every get-rich-quick scheme out there. But all I learned was that the conventional route was not going to get me anywhere.

I was working as a head bartender back then, but one night when I called in sick with pneumonia they fired me on the spot, even though I had a doctor's note! I was very angry. Up until this point, I'd always believed that I needed an employer to have an income. I had seen others start their own businesses, but I'd been too afraid to do the same. But I vowed from that point forward I would never rely on another employer again for income, and I never have since. In the face of uncertainty and fear, I started my own lawn-care service. Within a year, I was making more money part-time in charge of my own income than I'd ever made in my life. But my old programs and beliefs still made me think I had to do manual labor to create money—until I attended a seminar about building wealth through real estate investing. The leader promised to teach us how to build wealth if we bought his course, which seemed unconventional and pricey, but I overcame my fears and went for it. In hindsight, it was the smartest move I ever made.

Most people never live the lives they should. Old programs keep them stuck, and the core emotion that keeps them stuck is fear. Fear comes in three different forms. The first is complacency, when people make up excuses, like "I'm making $100,000 a year, that's good enough," or "I'm doing better than most." The next form of fear from people is the catatonic kind, in which they know what they should be doing but cannot bring themselves to do it. I taught tens of thousands of people about real estate investing and watched most of them do nothing, even with a home study course that told them exactly what to do. They could not get themselves to be proactive and take steps to achieve their desires. The last fear is disguised as a behavior: procrastination. People say, "Oh no, I'll get to that tomorrow," or "I'll invest when the market turns around." These are all just excuses to make people feel good about not living the life they dreamed of as a child. Students all across the world have asked me how to get past their fears. It is simple, but you're probably not going to like the answer: do what you fear most and your fear will disappear! I have done it and it works.

People ask me, "How can I become a millionaire?" Some think that if they become rich, they will be happy and have no problems. I can tell you from experience that this just isn't the case. True wealth is not just about money, but rather an equal combination of mind, body, relationship, and money. Now I will share the secret to building wealth in whatever business you choose, whether it's real estate, information marketing, or a medical practice. The one principle that will absolutely guarantee you success is: "Give others more value than you're asking for." When you create more value than the dollar amount you're asking the customer to pay, it becomes very easy for the customer to give you more money.

The next principle is getting comfortable with sales: selling and being sold something. Most of us grew up thinking anyone selling something was like a used car salesman trying to sell you a lemon. In my new program, I'm extremely comfortable with people selling to me. Wouldn't you want to have been sold the first McDonald's franchise or the first Apple stock option? Of course you don't know for sure what's going to happen, and you don't just accept everything either, but you can evaluate the opportunity and choose to move forward or pass on it. If you are not comfortable with selling, it's impossible for you to become wealthy. While I'm on the subject, I'll tell you that you are morally and ethically obligated to believe in what you're selling, or stop selling it immediately.

Before my mindset shift, I made the mistake whenever I met someone wealthy or successful, by approaching them and saying things like, "You're rich—can you give me some money or show me how to get rich?" I've since learned to come from a place of service first, by asking them, "What project or projects are you working on that I may be able to help you with?" I received an immediate positive response by restating it that way, and an incredible number of doors have opened for me.

If you want to make more money, then you must focus on it, and train your brain on a subconscious level to start thinking and speaking with a millionaire's mentality. When you focus on being 100% responsible for your situation and then creating a solution, your results are guaranteed as long as you stay the course and focus. Some people try to solve their problems and commit to achieving something for a short amount of time, but just before it's about to materialize they go back to old programs and habits and say, "This stuff doesn't work." Then the universal laws, true to form, respond by giving them what you said they want—proof that this stuff doesn't work. The Secret did a masterful job of bringing this principle to light, but some people missed or ignored one crucial piece of the law of attraction: you must take action! All good things materialize from it. So write this down: TAKE ACTION NOW! Start tending to the words and thoughts you use every day. That's an action plan that will cost you nothing, but produce unimaginable wealth.

You must take action now in order to create wealth. You might be filling up your day with things like taking out the trash, cleaning your house, mowing your lawn—examples of what I call minimum-wage work. If you spend your time doing this, you will be paid accordingly. I want you to continually ask yourself this question: What is the highest and best use of my time? What are you doing all day? Watching TV? Or chatting by the water cooler? See where you waste time, and start doing what I call "millionaire activities," like brainstorming money-making ideas, finding three new business contacts, and looking for problems with a business solution, to name a few.

Take this chapter: I'm giving you some of my best lessons and providing you with more value than what I'm asking of you. And I'm going to give you access to forty FREE hours of work from a virtual assistant (or VA), whose help can be used for anything you need to create or develop a business idea or service. My friend who owns a staffing company is providing this VA in the hopes that you will use the firm in the future. Simply go to www.va offer.com to redeem it.

It's been my great pleasure to share some of the strategies that have transformed my life and can transform yours. I'm going to give you one more very valuable item: for a limited time, you can get two free tickets to my seminar "Secrets of Subconscious Selling" (a $2,997 value) by visiting http://programmingconfidence.com/s3

If you would like to book Will "Power" Duquette to speak at an event, email Will@WillPowerDuquette.com, visit www.WillPowerDuquette.com, or call his office at (904) 260-9500.

About Will

Will "Power" Duquette, an internationally renowned hypnotist and a master of powerful communication and achievement, has been harnessing and tapping into the powers of the human mind since his own childhood. Duquette not only trains you in this mastery, he programs you to help guarantee your success in ALL areas, including mind, body, relationships, and building wealth fast! He calls this *Wealth Attraction Mastery!*

Like many people, Will Duquette came from very humble beginnings, but through dedication, education and hard work, he created financial freedom for himself. Will can help you create that very same success for yourself. He will tell you the truth about how to make money—he knows because he's done it from nothing! But it will take a few things from you: commitment, hard work, and the right tools and necessary mindset.

Through his control of the subconscious mind, Will Duquette turned his world around. He is now a respected business and personal consultant and a master trainer in human personal development programs. Today, Will is recognized as a leading expert in the skill areas of subconscious reprogramming and persuasion and influence, both of which are crucial to your success.

As a hypnotist, Will Duquette has entertained and educated audiences on stage for many years. He is the creator of the most powerful, funny and effective hypnotic stage show in the world! He has countless success stories of people just like you who have trained with him and transformed their lives forever. AND YOU CAN TOO! Come watch, learn and experience the often misunderstood power you all have within you, and learn how you too can achieve anything you set your mind to do, with the proper training from Will "Power" Duquette. Learn to take control of your own mind and your future.

Most people think they need more "how-to" information in order to build wealth, but this is simply not true. What they need is the proper mindset to achieve their dreams and goals, and this is exactly what Will Duquette can demonstrate.

Join Will "Power" Duquette and you will learn to create a millionaire mindset that will program you for a massive **SHIFT** in your life! Learn to conquer your fears and start taking actions TODAY towards what you know you should be doing. Become unstoppable, so that you can attract and build wealth more quickly and easily than EVER before. Double your income and live a rewarding and empowered life. Explode your self-confidence at will and commit to your success instantly. Will Duquette created a powerful and permanent shift in his life, and now he will show you how to create your own **personal power shift**, too. **Start TODAY!**

We'll see you at the show!

If you would like to book Will "Power" Duquette to speak at an event, email Will@WillPowerDuquette.com, visit www.WillPowerDuquette.com, or call his office at (904) 260-9500.

CHAPTER 15

Business Partnerships: Making the Marriage Work

By Hugh O. Stewart

A bad business partnership is a lot like a bad marriage. When personalities clash, and goals are at cross purposes, the conflicts can quickly tear apart the bonds that held you together in the first place.

An example:

Along with my business partner at the time, I teamed up with a married couple to form a real estate partnership that seemed like the greatest thing in the world for the first two years. For those first two years, we generated significant revenue. As a part-time business, we completed between five and twelve transactions a year and had a clear deal structure in place that worked for all involved.

Then the couple had an opportunity for a really big deal and wanted us to be partners in the new business. After everything had gone so well, how could we say no? We kept the same financial structure in place and jumped in.

And that's where everything started to go wrong.

This new deal created a very different financial situation that forced us to work much more for far less—actually, for nothing at all, because we received no operational compensation. Yes, we were supposed to split the profits evenly, but it rapidly became clear that there weren't going to be any, and all we had was the existing equity.

My partner and I grew resentful of the fact that the couple had repeatedly gone off to work on projects of their own that made them money without bringing us any results. The couple also became resentful that we were making demands on their time for very little immediate benefit, and they didn't want to hear our concerns. They had to feed their family. When it became clear that the partnership had nowhere to go, we decided to split the assets and move on.

That's when the couple's attorney presented me with a $95,000 lawsuit—after I'd already lost $150,000 in the previous six months.

We settled for a lot less than the $95,000, but my partner and I were stuck operating a ruined asset that we didn't have the skills or talent to run. The experience sucked all the joy and vitality out of us for a while, not to mention a lot of business capital.

What went wrong? Well, all of us lost our sense of perspective—and our respect for each other's positions. When we shifted to the new deal, we all looked backward rather than forward, and didn't protect ourselves against the new intricacies of the financial arrangements. When the partnership went sour, we pointed fingers instead of amicably working towards a fair resolution for all parties.

But it doesn't have to have to be this way.

In 2007, I had been working successfully with the abovementioned business partner for about five years, he told me he was going to retire in two years (he's 32 years older than I am). Instead of prompting panic in either of us, this conversation gave us the time and the luxury to have a series of very cool and dynamic discussions on how our roles and our financial arrangements would change over the next 24 months.

Since April 1, 2009, his announced retirement date, he has exited the operations of virtually all of our jointly-owned businesses. We were able to preserve our business relationship, as well as our personal one.

In one particular business, we were even able to grow in an industry that was shrinking. As a matter of fact, we recently sold that business for many times what we originally paid for it. Yes, we had a few conflicts along the way—but these were always *business* conflicts, not personal ones, and we resolved them quickly and efficiently.

That's because we respected each other and wanted to be *fair* with each other. And these are the keys to a successful business partnership.

BUSINESS PARTNERSHIPS: THE BIG PICTURE

I've been involved in nine business partnerships over the years, three of which ended well, three okay, and three badly. I've learned a great deal from these experiences, which is why I'm able to provide valuable advice to my clients on how they can profit from these kinds of pairings—and how they can work through the inevitable personal and professional speed bumps along the way. I'd like to share a little of that advice in this chapter.

Any business venture is a gamble to some degree. Partnerships will instantly double the ante on all fronts. Yes, you have twice the resources and business skills to put into the pot, but you also have twice the potential for drama and rancor in your life.

Statistics vary, but it's usually estimated that about 70% to 80% of all business partnerships fail. The good news, however, is that there are steps you can take to make a partnership a smart bet that pays off for everyone concerned—as long as all parties approach that partnership in the right spirit.

That spirit has to do with the concept of fairness, which you need to apply to your partners as well as yourself. It extends to how much people are getting paid, how hard everyone is working, and how everyone perceives the partnership is functioning (or not functioning). Engaging in consistent communication and actively adjusting for changing circumstances will always allow the process to work as well as possible.

PUT PARTNERSHIPS TO THE TEST—
BEFORE STARTING ONE

Because I have been through my share of misfortunes in business partnerships, I've learned to ask myself several crucial questions while
considering whether to enter into another:

- How far do I want to progress in the next three years—both
personally and professionally? What level of growth would
make me happy?

- Am I with people who can grow with me to that level?

- Do these people have the backing, resources and ability to
help enable that growth?

- Are their goals and dreams in tune with my own?

The answers to these questions have to be honest ones. It's important
that you lay down a strong foundation for a business relationship at
this juncture—feeling good about where it will take you is critical to
providing you with both the motivation and inspiration to give it your
all.

If those broad questions generate positive answers, it's time to drill
deeper. You should now define exactly what your role in the new
partnership will be, and what *you* are bringing to the new venture.
Most people only focus on what they will *get* out of the new business
relationship, but you must clarify your contributions as well.

Ideally, partnerships should mean that all parties are bringing equal
value to the table in some fashion (business capital, connections,
needed skills, and so on) to create something bigger than the sum of
its parts. If you can't deliver on your end, it will inevitably cause problems at some point.

THE T.O.S. CONCEPT

Next, you and your potential partner should tackle what I call "The
T.O.S. Concept." T.O.S. stands for Threats, Opportunities and

Strengths - the three most important areas you should explore as they pertain to you, the other party or parties, and the proposed partnership itself.

Dealing directly beforehand with the issues that T.O.S. can generate will lay the groundwork for a productive shared future together built on trust. This is because powerful emotions inform each of the three areas, and emotions are ultimately what can pull a partnership together or tear it apart.

- **Threats**

  In this area, you want to identify as specifically as possible what events or activities you're trying to prevent within this partnership. Fear is a destructive element in any enterprise, and it can cause paranoia, distrust and angry accusations. Write out or talk through the future potential threats to your partnership and find agreement on how you will address them.

- **Opportunities**

  This is about excitement. Discover, list and explore the business opportunities that would be exciting for the business to engage in. In this exercise, imagine that you won't have any limitations or restrictions (especially those that you listed in the previous section). See which opportunities bring about the most personal excitement and passion for each group member, and then decide which ones to focus on the most.

- **Strengths**

  What are each person's main strengths in terms of the potential partnership? Identify and list them, and consider how they will create and contribute to everyone's overall confidence in the partnership. This confidence will see you through rocky times and help you excel in good times. Its existence is vital if you want to avoid panicked overreactions to both threats and opportunities.

And remember again: this process is just as much about you as it is the other partners involved. I often find myself chuckling when people complain to me about their partners, when the truth is that the complainer is actually a source of the problem. This isn't to say that these people have intentionally created problems, but rather that they haven't directly expressed to the partner what they really want out of the relationship, and they're unclear as to what their roles and responsibilities are in the business.

VETTING YOUR PARTNER

Everything I've just described pertains to the operation of the business partnership. Now it's time to get a little more personal.

As I said at the start, a business partnership closely resembles a marriage. In both cases, if you enter into the relationship with the wrong person, disaster is going to strike—no matter how many ground rules in place beforehand.

Now, when I say "the wrong person," I'm not talking about someone who has a different background or life experiences. The odds that are your partner will differ from you in some respects, which an advantage in that you both have a wider pool of knowledge and experiences to draw from. What you do have to ensure, though, is that your vision for business and life is not in direct conflict with your potential partner's vision.

For example, there is the matter of **core personal beliefs**. Can the two of you work together without these beliefs clashing? This isn't as trivial as you might think. I remember the time that someone told me that because I did not believe in God the same way he did, my skills were of no value to the potential partnership. There's no real way to resolve a conflict like that.

That incident did, however, teach me a good lesson. I used to think that those kinds of beliefs had nothing to do with trying to run a business with someone. When someone's beliefs are that ingrained and they conflict with your core values, this conflict will eventually cause problems.

You also don't want to find yourself joined at the hip to someone with a **distracting family situation** that somehow conflicts with the workings of the partnership. A messy divorce or an insistence that the partnership employ a spouse or relative who's not a good fit can create unpleasant disagreements that spill over into the professional operation of the partnership. Sometimes these issues aren't really that serious, but you must be *absolutely sure* they are repeatedly monitored and discussed in order to avoid divisive conflict.

Going beyond personalities and values, you should also fully investigate your potential partner's **paper trail**. This goes beyond trust issues to vital practical ones that affect the basics of being able to do business. Soon after I started one partnership, I found out that we had to apply for certain federal and state licenses just to operate. The application process required full background checks of each major and minor partner; I even had to attest to the "moral uprightness" of each of my partners. Luckily, our background checks came back clear—but you don't want to risk an unpleasant surprise. Needless to say, it would have been disastrous to discover that my partner hadn't cleared those checks at that point in the relationship.

That's why you need to know certain things about your partner from the beginning. Run a comprehensive background check that includes his or her criminal history, lawsuits, judgments, liens, bankruptcies, property ownership, address history, relatives and associates, and marriage or divorce records. You will also need to know about any of their other business endeavors that may affect your shared operations. There are many websites that offer background reports. Your partner can either provide you with one or you can run one on him or her using his or her Social Security Number and signed authorization. (You, of course, should provide the same kind of report to him or her.) Your partner may be reluctant to share this information with you, but he or she should be made to understand its importance to the business itself. Make it clear that it's a professional matter.

By the way, business licenses aren't the only thing affected by a partner's background. If you're looking to open a corporate or partnership bank account, obtain business credit or "key man" insurance, or even win a government contract, everyone applying will have to provide a credit report. That's why, in addition to the background check, you also need to run credit reports, including a FICO credit score, for all partners.

Finally, the suitability of a partner can come down to one last question: **can you trust this person?** And, just as crucially, can he or she trust you? Do you feel comfortable being open and honest with him or her? Would you be willing to tell this person everything about what's going on with the business, even if it might reflect poorly on you for some reason? Or would you be tempted to hide little things—or even leave him or her out of the loop entirely when important issues come up?

Building and maintaining trust levels is crucial in building a successful partnership.

There's a great deal more you need to know if:

1. You are thinking about entering into a business partnership.

2. You want to improve the partnership that you are already in.

3. You are ready to dissolve your current partnership.

It is important to make decisions early about issues like the right business structure, compensation arrangements, the maintaining of relationships, and, finally, the amicable and fair dissolution of the partnership after it has run its course. If you'd like to learn more about business partnerships and how to ensure their success, I invite you to visit my website at www.partnershipmaximizer.com.

Business partnerships have opened up whole new worlds of industry and brightened many a profit picture. Your business partnership can be this rewarding as well, if you approach it with the right spirit—and keep asking and answering the right questions.

About Hugh

Hugh O. Stewart has amassed great knowledge in the creation and operation of extremely successful business ventures. He has developed and operated over seventeen businesses in the past decade, in industries including financial services, real estate, advertising, insurance consulting and coaching.

Building successful businesses as partnerships is an exceptional way to build wealth, and Hugh has a great deal of experience in that arena as well. He has been involved in nine partnerships— from joint ventures and equity sharing to nonprofit—granting him a deeper understanding of how to create and maintain business relationships that benefit all parties.

To share his knowledge for how to build outstanding companies with business owners, Hugh developed the Confident Solutions Coach Program. Using his expertise in building business operational systems, hiring exceptional talent, and helping business owners structure their businesses to allow them to be less involved in the day-to-day operations, his unique coaching methods and products have helped many people to realize the success they desire.

Learn more about Hugh Stewart and the successful methods of the Confident Solutions Coach by visiting www.ConfidentSolutionsCoach.com.